Tony Kushner's plays includ ... *Room Called Day*; *Hydriotaphia*; *Angels in America, Parts One and Two*; *Slavs!* and *Homebody/Kabul*. His adaptations include Corneille's *The Illusion*, Ansky's *A Dybbuk*, Brecht's *The Good Person of Szechuan*, Goethe's *Stella* and English-language libretti for two operas: Krasa's *Brundibar* and Martinu's *Comedy on the Bridge*. In 2003, HBO presented a film version of *Angels in America*, directed by Mike Nichols. *Homebody/Kabul* is being adapted for film by Mira Nair. Recent books include *Brundibar*, a picture book for children, illustrated by Maurice Sendak; *The Art of Maurice Sendak, 1980–The Present* and *Wrestling with Zion: Progressive Jewish-American Responses to the Israeli-Palestinian Conflict*, co-edited with Alisa Solomon.

Mr. Kushner is the recipient of numerous awards, including the Pulitzer Prize for Drama (*Angels in America, Part One*), two Tony Awards for Best Play (*Angels in America*, 1993 and 1994), three Obie Awards (*Slavs!*, *Homebody/Kabul* and *Caroline, or Change*), an Evening Standard Award (*Angels in America*), two Dramatists Guild/Hull-Warriner Awards (*Angels in America* and *Homebody/Kabul*), an Arts Award from the American Academy of Arts and Letters, a Cultural Achievement Award from the National Foundation for Jewish Culture, the PEN/Laura Pels Award for Mid-Career Playwright and a Spirit of Justice Award from the Gay and Lesbian Advocates and Defenders. He was born in Lake Charles, Louisiana, but he doesn't live there anymore.

OTHER BOOKS BY
TONY KUSHNER

ANGELS IN AMERICA, PART ONE:
MILLENNIUM APPROACHES

ANGELS IN AMERICA, PART TWO:
PERESTROIKA

A BRIGHT ROOM CALLED DAY

DEATH & TAXES: HYDRIOTAPHIA & OTHER PLAYS

A DYBBUK AND OTHER TALES OF THE SUPERNATURAL
Adapted from S. Ansky
with translations by Joachim Neugroschel

HOMEBODY/KABUL

THE ILLUSION
Freely adapted from Pierre Corneille

THINKING ABOUT THE LONGSTANDING PROBLEMS
OF VIRTUE AND HAPPINESS
Essays, a Play, two Poems and a Prayer

CAROLINE,
or CHANGE

A MUSICAL

Book and Lyrics by
Tony Kushner

Music by
Jeanine Tesori

NICK HERN BOOKS
LONDON
www.nickhernbooks.co.uk

A Nick Hern Book

Caroline, or Change first published in Great Britain as a paperback original
in 2006 by Nick Hern Books Limited, 14 Larden Road, London W3 7ST
by special arrangement with Theatre Communications Group, Inc., New York

Caroline, or Change copyright © 1998, 2001, 2003, 2004 by Tony Kushner

Book design by Lisa Govan
Front cover art and design by Paul Davis

Printed and bound in Great Britain by Bookmarque, Croydon, Surrey

A CIP catalogue record for this book is available from the British Library

ISBN-13 978 1 85459 948 3
ISBN-10 1 85459 948 8

This play is for Maudie Lee Davis

ACKNOWLEDGMENTS

Caroline began as a commission by San Francisco Opera under the leadership of Lotfi Mansouri, and I am grateful to him, and to Kip Cranna, for their enthusiasm, their support and their incredible expansive far-sighted generosity.

All collaborative art forms are difficult, and musicals are collaborative to the *nth* degree, and hugely expensive besides, and working on a musical is a little like trying to steer an ocean liner with a rusty rudder through an obstacle course of icebergs in a typhoon. The playwright/lyricist/librettist/book writer wishes to thank the people who kept this enterprise from foundering.

John Dias was the play's first and best champion and he kept us on track from the beginning. The Public Theater was its first home, and I am indebted to every one of its hardworking, courageous staff: Michael Hurst, Mara Manus, Seth Shepsle, Rebecca Rugg, Joe Levy, Niegel Smith, and the ever-incredible Irene Cabrera. Our cast was assembled with loving care and dedication by Jordan Thaler and Heidi Griffiths.

Caroline opened at The Public because Carole Shorenstein Hays made it financially possible, with help from Freddy DeMann. When doom threatens, Carole calls and incants a spell, and doom dispels. Our further life, the move to Broadway and all our growing as we moved, we owe to our fearless and unstoppable hero/producers, who disregarded the usual signs, portents, readings of tea leaves and goat entrails, and even put aside their own hard-won business acumen to invest, purely, because they felt *Caroline* merited a life beyond its initial run. So thanks and kudos and weepy weak-kneed gratitude to Carole and Freddy and (alphabetically) also Jane Bergère, Roger Berlind; Kristin Caskey and Mike Isaacson of Fox Theatricals, the late Joan Cullman, Ruth Hendel, Greg Holland; Rocco Landesman, Paul Libin and Jack Viertel of the Jujamcyn organization, Margo Lion, Jennifer Manocherian, Elisabeth Morten, Scott Nederlander, Daryl Roth, Scott Rudin, Jeffrey Sine, Cheryl Wiesenfeld and Fred Zollo—modern-day Medicis, all of them, but much nicer and more hands-on (in a productive way). Keri Putnam, Richard Plepler, Kary Antholis, Glenn Whitehead and especially Colin Callender of HBO Films made my year and changed my life. Rocco, Jack and Margo, unphased by the sniffers and the mickey-mockers, rode in immediately to the rescue.

Stuart Thompson, our general manager, has been an island of tranquil competence and passionate devotion in otherwise stormy seas, and Chris Boneau and Amy Jacobs have protected us from many terrors of the deep. The luminous Helen Bing made an important contribution. Paul Davis gave us a beautiful portrait.

Riccardo Hernández and Paul Tazewell made smart and gorgeous sets and costumes for us, and Jules Fisher and Peggy Eisenhauer did their usual lighting miracles. The playwright thanks Jules for his habit of encouragement. Jon Weston figured out how to make it sound beautiful downtown and uptown, and Patrick Pummill made it sound beautiful night after night.

This is a script, not a cast album, but it's impossible to write a list of thank yous without naming *Caroline*'s musical heart and soul: Joseph Joubert and Rick Bassett, two of the show's amazing orchestrators; Kimberly Grigsby, our brilliant musical supervisor; and Linda Twine, our magnificent conductor; as well as our orchestra: Steve Bargonetti, Ben Brown, Chris Cardona, John Clancy, Dave Creswell, Paul Garment, Matthew Sklar, Shane Shanahan, Stephen Wisner, Anja Wood and Paul Woodiel.

Rick Steiger is an adorable genius of a stage manager, and Lisa Dawn Cave and Kevin Bertolacci are also adorable and indispensable and without the three of them the whole caboodle would have sunk straight to the bottom.

That there is a cast album, *Caroline*'s purchase against oblivion, has most of all to do with Freddie Gershon of MTI, who jumped in all alone at the show's darkest moment and saved the day, or at least the spirits of the show's composer and librettist, and who helped make the recording possible. We're also grateful to the point of babbling for the courage, generosity and savvy of Hollywood Records' Glen Lajeski, Mitchell Leib, Monica Zierhut, Steve Fickinger, Bill Rosenfield and Bob Schaper.

Buryl Red, orchestrator, has been *Caroline*'s guardian angel from the moment Jeanine and I began working together.

My assistant, Antonia Nike Grilikhes-Lasky, was tireless, smart and invaluable throughout the process. Joyce Ketay and Nancy Rose, amazing agents, negotiated the impossible and navigated their clients through treacherous shoals.

Jeanine undoubtedly has her own gratitude to express to Michael Rafter, her husband, and Siena Rafter, her daughter—but this is a book and so I get to use this space to express my own gratitude to them for their expertise (Michael) and support (Michael and Siena), and to apologize to them both for needing so much of Jeanine's time and attention.

Kimberly T. Flynn and I have had many discussions, political, psychological, and we shared memories of Louisiana, all of which informed the script.

Oskar Eustis provided invaluable dramaturgical advice as always, and oceans of emotional support.

I'm grateful to my family: my father, Bill, who was and is the true wellspring of my music, and who unlike poor grief-stricken Stuart Gellman was and is a great father and a great man; and my brother Eric and my sister Lesley, for their love, for their enthusiasm and support, for corroboration and for having lived our Lake Charles childhood together. My aunt Martha Deutscher has been as always a champion.

Acknowledgements

Thanks to Maurice Sendak for approving, and for the moon. My husband, Mark Harris, has been a great help, dispenser of sterling advice, keeper of the flame, as he always is; but he has a particular love for *Caroline*, and he suffered through every second of this with me. Dr. Harriet Harris, Mark's mother, read the play in its first draft, just before her death, and she liked it.

And, of course, finally, my infinite love and gratitude to and for the cast of *Caroline, or Change*, and to and for Jeanine and George, most of all.

INTRODUCTION

Caroline, or Change tells a story I've been thinking about for
many years. It's partly based on an incident from my childhood,
grounded in memories from my early life. I wanted to write
about race relations, the civil rights movement, and African-
Americans and southern Jews in the early 1960s, a time of
protean change sweeping the country—and to write about these
things from the perspective of a small, somewhat isolated
southern town. I grew up in Lake Charles, Louisiana, during
this period. Change was taking place in Lake Charles, of course,
but in a more subterranean fashion, and at a different pace, than
elsewhere in America. I took notes over the years and dredged
up various recollections, but I couldn't find the right vessel for
the story I had decided to tell.

I decided to write *Caroline* when San Francisco Opera asked
me to do a libretto. I am an ardent opera fan, and I come from
a musical family: my parents and my brother are professional
musicians. I think getting a commission from an opera company
made it possible for me to begin the play. Since I would be
writing lyrics, I had permission to write . . . well, lyrically, to use
a loosely rhythmic, loosely rhymed verse instead of prose. And
writing text for an opera connected the story I wanted to tell to
music, a central component of my childhood, and perhaps the
missing key to my memory of these characters, these incidents,
that time.

I brought the first draft of *Caroline* to George C. Wolfe, hoping he'd help me as I developed the script, and hoping also that he'd want to direct it. George agreed to work on the project, but he felt that the dramatic demands of the material would require a cast of singing actors rather than opera singers. He suggested that we turn it into a musical-theater piece. San Francisco Opera's intended composer, meanwhile, decided he didn't want to write an opera after all, and so George and I began to search for a theater composer. Our first choice was Jeanine Tesori; we both loved her musical, *Violet*, and her score for Nick Hytner's production of *Twelfth Night*. Jeanine turned us down, for a variety of reasons. She felt the script was too complete, assuming I wouldn't do rewrites—this was before we'd met.

George and I, disappointed, spent another year looking for a composer, not agreeing on or even finding any other suitable candidate. Then Jeanine and I were asked to collaborate on a score for a musical based on a film. I agreed because I love musicals. I have always wanted to try writing one; also there was the promise of good money. And I wanted to work with Jeanine. We wrote a couple of songs together, she realized that I like rewriting, we realized we liked each other, we realized we didn't care much for the adaptation we were supposed to be doing, at which point I proposed that she take another look at *Caroline*.

George, Jeanine and I spent four years making *Caroline, or Change*. I have never enjoyed a partnership more, nor have I ever felt prouder of the results. My collaborators' vast experience with musical-theater has been essential to the shaping of the piece, compensating for my embarrassing awkwardness in a medium in which I can claim nothing in the way of expertise. Writing a musical felt to me like starting over as a writer, like writing my first page of dialogue, writing my first play, waiting for the Fraudulence Police to kick down the door and break my pencil.

The project began with my libretto, and I have always worked alone as a playwright until now; I'm a reasonably friendly person but I've never felt an urge to co-author anything. But the script you are about to read has changed since the first draft. The words are mine, the music is Jeanine's, but responsibility for the final shape of both words and music can't be neatly allocated.

Ours is by leagues my most intimate working collaboration, and the most pleasurable and productive; we've shaped each others' work on the piece in an atmosphere of an almost preposterous harmony. It's required struggle and effort—a lot of that—but also real joy.

George C. Wolfe is incomparable, astonishing, utterly brilliant, utterly original, and very brave. I already knew from our production of *Angels in America* on Broadway how smart he is about dramatic structure, language, the human heart, political struggle. I've learned through *Caroline* that he has an exquisite musical ear.

I'm enormously excited about having written a musical. I intend to remain a playwright, but I hope I'll continue growing as a lyricist and writer of musicals as well. In the workshops we did, in watching George work with the fantastic singer / actors we gathered together—and *Caroline* has had an unbelievable cast, starting with the great Tonya Pinkins in the title role (when I brought the script to George he said, "I know who can play this, I know who you wrote this part for!")—in my long sessions with Jeanine, I've learned hugely important things, I suppose primarily about the relationship of sound and sense, the emotional and the rational. There are places inside us only song can reach. Words can do all sorts of things; obviously I'm a big big fan of words, of speech, of language. Words can say what words can't say; the apt description can describe the indescribable.

But as someone who has spent his adult lifetime trying to move audiences with words alone, I have advice to offer any playwright who cares about such things: try a musical. Words betray the arduousness of the struggle to express, to interpret, to understand. Music offers up emotion and idea with an organicity and shapeliness and spontaneity that must be what we mean when we say that something possesses grace. Words can be graceful, but music is grace itself. Music is a blessing that enters the soul through the ear.

Of course you have to find the right composer. Jeanine has that rare knack of writing a tune that makes all the doors and windows of the heart fly open and all sorts of weather rush in, I think she has that Italian opera gene, I think I was very smart to find a composer whose name ends in a vowel, I'm a huge opera queen and so I knew: Donizetti Rossini Bellini Verdi Puccini—look for the vowel at the end of the name! My mother, Sylvia Deutscher Kushner, who was a great bassoonist, used to play in the pit for New York City Opera; she told me she always hated performances of *Madama Butterfly*, because it's hard to play the bassoon when you're sobbing.

My little niece, Ciara, who lives in Vienna, has listened all her young life to opera. My brother Eric is first horn of the Wiener Symphoniker, and so Ciara has heard great operas since she was embryonic: Wagner, Verdi, Massenet, Schoenberg, Tchaikovsky. But recently the Wiener Symphoniker played *West Side Story*. Now we sing Tony and Maria duets together, Ciara and I. She's six, she lives in Vienna, she knows nothing of New York nor of American racial strife nor, as is appropriate for any six-year-old, much about strife, period. So why did *West Side Story* appeal to her so indelibly, so instantaneously, and why is she now running about singing *My Fair Lady* and *Oklahoma*? Watching her, I remembered the early and overwhelmingly powerful spell these shows cast for me. By my tenth birthday I'd learned the scores of *Damn Yankees* and *The Mikado* note by note, word by word, from the overture on.

I recently heard the New York Philharmonic do a concert version of *Sweeney Todd* for Stephen Sondheim's seventieth birthday. The entire audience of jaded, battle-weary adult New Yorkers levitated out of their seats, borne aloft on a cloud of compound vapor in which terror and glee and sheer sensual delight were indescribably and perfectly blended; it was ecstasy, pure and simple, and we've all felt it, in the presence of great musical-theater. Six years old or six hundred, it's instantly recognizable: Bacchic joy, as close to irresistible and universal as almost anything other than Shakespeare or Mozart.

Caroline returns, in this volume, to something resembling its nascent condition—silence. Here is what the play alone has to offer, apart from the occasion it has provided for the composition of glorious music—the play alone, having passed through that occasion and having been profoundly changed by it.

The text has been transformed, but the core of *Caroline* has, like its title character, resisted change. This play comes from sorrow, from anger and grief, and also from hope learned from history, from recent history, which has shown us both the terrors and also the pleasures of change, which has shown us that change, progress, is difficult, uneven, uncertain, but also absolutely possible. Sorrow, anger and grief, our tragedies, shouldn't blind us to our victories. The failure of this country to address racism and poverty, domestically and globally, has been a terrible failure, its cost incalculable, and the worst consequences have not yet arrived. And yet the African-American civil rights movement changed not only America but the entire world. A new model for human liberation was born of that movement, of that moment, a model that oppressed people around the world have embraced. And the struggle goes on. Jewish-Americans, with their deep understanding of the vital role of the federal government in protecting minority rights, with their deep commitment to social and economic justice, were and are critically important participants in the struggle. If the movement's mightiest dreams haven't been realized yet, it would be worse than a mistake to predict that they never shall be realized. If that epic struggle did not accomplish everything it intended, it breached the wall of oppression, and through that breach the future is pouring in.

Tony Kushner
New York City
June 2004

CAROLINE, or CHANGE

PRODUCTION HISTORY

Caroline, or Change was part of The Public Theater's New Work Now! reading series in May 1999, in New York City (George C. Wolfe, Producer; Mara Manus, Executive Director). It was directed by the author. The dramaturg was John Dias. Casting was provided by Jordan Thaler and Heidi Griffiths. The production coordinator was Carol Clark.

CAROLINE THIBODEAUX	Rosalyn Coleman
THE WASHING MACHINE	Noel True
THE RADIO/THE MOON	Ann Duquesnay
NOAH GELLMAN	Adam Lamberg
THE DRYER/THE BUS	Chuck Cooper
GRANDMA GELLMAN	Sloane Shelton
GRANDPA GELLMAN	Ben Hammer
ROSE STOPNICK GELLMAN	Carrie Preston
STUART GELLMAN	Dan Futterman
DOTTY MOFFETT	Michael Hyatt
EMMIE THIBODEAUX	Afi McClendon
MR. STOPNICK	David Margulies
HEAD OF THE STATUE OF THE CONFEDERATE SOLDIER	J. R. Horne
STAGE DIRECTIONS	Terrell Tilford

The play received a subsequent, private but important, reading in August 2000.

CAROLINE THIBODEAUX	Tonya Pinkins
DOTTY MOFFETT/THE WASHING MACHINE	Michael Hyatt
THE RADIO/THE MOON	Ann Duquesnay
NOAH GELLMAN	Adam Lamberg
THE DRYER/THE BUS	Tommy Hollis
GRANDMA GELLMAN	Lola Pashalinski
GRANDPA GELLMAN	Bill Buell
ROSE STOPNICK GELLMAN	Carrie Preston
STUART GELLMAN	Ben Shenkman
EMMIE THIBODEAUX	Pascale Armand
MR. STOPNICK	David Margulies
HEAD OF THE STATUE OF THE CONFEDERATE SOLDIER	J. R. Horne
STAGE DIRECTIONS	Angela Hughes

With the score for the first act composed, *Caroline, or Change* was given a developmental workshop at The Public Theater from August 5–17, 2001. It was directed by George C. Wolfe. The musical consultant was Kimberly Grigsby, the stage manager was Rick Steiger and the assistant stage manager was Lisa Dawn Cave.

CAROLINE THIBODEAUX	Tonya Pinkins
THE WASHING MACHINE	Capathia Jenkins
THE RADIO	Ramona Keller
THE RADIO	Tracy Nicole Chapman
THE RADIO	Marva Hicks
NOAH GELLMAN	Jonathan Press
THE DRYER/THE BUS	Chuck Cooper
GRANDMA GELLMAN	Alice Playten

GRANDPA GELLMAN/ HEAD OF THE STATUE OF THE CONFEDERATE SOLDIER	Reathel Bean
ROSE STOPNICK GELLMAN	Veanne Cox
STUART GELLMAN	Denis O'Hare
DOTTY MOFFETT	Kimberly JaJuan
THE MOON	Priscilla Baskerville
EMMIE THIBODEAUX	Anika Noni Rose
JACKIE THIBODEAUX	Jason Dendy
JOE THIBODEAUX	Sean Taylor
MR. STOPNICK	David Margulies

The musical, both acts composed, received another developmental workshop at The Public Theater from October 14–November 1, 2002, under the direction of George C. Wolfe. The musical consultant was Kimberly Grigsby, casting was provided by Jordan Thaler and Heidi Griffiths, the dramaturg was Rebecca Rugg, the production stage manager was Rick Steiger, the stage manager was Gwen Gilliam and the production assistant was Aquaila Barnes. On Location Education: Jodi Green (supervisor), Sherryl Marshall (tutor), Stephanie Summerville (wrangler).

CAROLINE THIBODEAUX	Tonya Pinkins
THE WASHING MACHINE	Capathia Jenkins
THE RADIO	Ramona Keller
THE RADIO	Tracy Nicole Chapman
THE RADIO	Marva Hicks
NOAH GELLMAN	Harrison Chad
THE DRYER/THE BUS	Chuck Cooper
GRANDMA GELLMAN	Alice Playten
GRANDPA GELLMAN/ HEAD OF THE STATUE OF THE CONFEDERATE SOLDIER	Reathel Bean
ROSE STOPNICK GELLMAN	Veanne Cox
STUART GELLMAN	Denis O'Hare

DOTTY MOFFETT	Chandra Wilson
THE MOON	Priscilla Baskerville
EMMIE THIBODEAUX	Anika Noni Rose
JACKIE THIBODEAUX	Sean Taylor
JOE THIBODEAUX	Jeremy Meleek Leggett
MR. STOPNICK	David Margulies

A final workshop was given by The Public from May 27–June 20, 2003, under the direction of George C. Wolfe. The music coordinator was Kimberly Grigsby, the conductor was Linda Twine, casting was provided by Jordan Thaler and Heidi Griffiths, the dramaturg was Rebecca Rugg, the production stage manager was Rick Steiger, the assistant stage manager was Lisa Dawn Cave and the production assistant was Kevin Bertolacci. On Location Education: Jodi Green (supervisor), Irene Karasik (tutor), Victoria Haynes (wrangler).

CAROLINE THIBODEAUX	Tonya Pinkins
THE WASHING MACHINE	Capathia Jenkins
THE RADIO	Stacy Francis
THE RADIO	Tracy Nicole Chapman
THE RADIO	Marva Hicks
NOAH GELLMAN	Harrison Chad
THE DRYER/THE BUS	Chuck Cooper
GRANDMA GELLMAN	Alice Playten
GRANDPA GELLMAN/	
HEAD OF THE STATUE OF	
THE CONFEDERATE SOLDIER	Reathel Bean
ROSE STOPNICK GELLMAN	Veanne Cox
STUART GELLMAN	Adam Grupper
DOTTY MOFFETT	Chandra Wilson
THE MOON	Barbara Conrad
EMMIE THIBODEAUX	Anika Noni Rose
JACKIE THIBODEAUX	Chevon Rutty
JOE THIBODEAUX	Phil Harris
MR. STOPNICK	David Margulies

Caroline, or Change premiered in November 2003 at The Public Theater (George C. Wolfe, Producer; Mara Manus, Executive Director) in New York City. It was directed by George C. Wolfe. The scenic design was by Riccardo Hernández; the costume design was by Paul Tazewell; the lighting design was by Jules Fisher and Peggy Eisenhauer; the sound design was by Jon Weston; the hair design was by Jeffrey Frank; the choreography was by Hope Clarke, the orchestrations were by Rick Bassett, Joseph Joubert and Buryl Red; the music supervisor was Kimberly Grigsby; the music director and conductor was Linda Twine; the production stage manager was Rick Steiger; and the stage manager was Lisa Dawn Cave.

CAROLINE THIBODEAUX	Tonya Pinkins
THE WASHING MACHINE	Capathia Jenkins
THE RADIO	Tracy Nicole Chapman, Marva Hicks, Ramona Keller
NOAH GELLMAN	Harrison Chad
THE DRYER	Chuck Cooper
GRANDMA GELLMAN	Alice Playten
GRANDPA GELLMAN	Reathel Bean
ROSE STOPNICK GELLMAN	Veanne Cox
STUART GELLMAN	David Costabile
DOTTY MOFFETT	Chandra Wilson
THE MOON	Adriane Lenox
THE BUS	Chuck Cooper
EMMIE THIBODEAUX	Anika Noni Rose
JACKIE THIBODEAUX	Kevin Ricardo Tate
JOE THIBODEAUX	Marcus Carl Franklin
MR. STOPNICK	Larry Keith
THE STATUE OF THE CONFEDERATE SOLDIER	Reathel Bean

On May 2, 2004, The Public Theater's production of *Caroline, or Change* opened on Broadway at the Eugene O'Neill Theatre with the same artistic team, except for these changes: the role of The Moon was performed by Aisha de Haas and the role of Jackie Thibodeaux was performed by Leon G. Thomas III. It was produced by Carole Shorenstein Hays, HBO Films, Jujamcyn Theaters, Freddy DeMann, Scott Rudin, Hendel/ Morten/ Wiesenfeld, Fox Theatricals/Manocherian/Bergère, Roger Berlind, Clear Channel Entertainment, Joan Cullman, Greg Holland/Scott Nederlander, Margo Lion, Daryl Roth, Zollo/ Sine, in association with The Public Theater, and with support from Helen and Peter Bing and Theatre Development Fund.

On October 18, 2006, the National Theatre's production of *Caroline, or Change* premiered in the UK at the Lyttelton Theatre. It was directed by George C Wolfe; the choreographer was Hope Clarke; the set designer was Riccardo Hernández; the lighting designers were Jules Fisher and Peggy Eisenhauer; and the costume designer was Paul Tazewell. The conductor and music supervisor was Martin Lowe; orchestrations were by Rick Bassett, Joseph Joubert and Buryl Red; the associate music director was Mark Etherington. The cast was as follows:

CAROLINE THIBODEAUX	Tonya Pinkins
THE WASHING MACHINE	Malinda Parris
THE RADIO	Ramona Keller
	Joy Malcolm
	Nataylia Roni
NOAH GELLMAN	Greg Bernstein
	Perry Millward
	Jonny Weldon
THE DRYER / THE BUS	Clive Rowe
GRANDMA GELLMAN	Valda Aviks
GRANDPA GELLMAN	Ian Lavender
ROSE STOPNICK GELLMAN	Anna Francolini
STUART GELLMAN	Richard Henders
DOTTY MOFFETT	Nora Cole
THE MOON	Angela M Caesar
EMMIE THIBODEAUX	Pippa Bennett-Warner
MR. STOPNICK	Hilton McRae
JACKIE / JOE THIBODEAUX	Kazim Benson
	Ronald Chabvuica
	Louis Ekoku
	Kuan Frye
	Jamal Hope
	Mitchell Zhangazha

CHARACTERS

CAROLINE THIBODEAUX,
works for the Gellmans, thirty-nine years old

THE WASHING MACHINE

THE RADIO

NOAH GELLMAN, son of Stuart Gellman, eight years old

THE DRYER

GRANDMA GELLMAN, Noah's grandmother, Stuart's mother

GRANDPA GELLMAN, Noah's grandfather, Stuart's father

ROSE STOPNICK GELLMAN,
recently married to Stuart, mid-to-late thirties

STUART GELLMAN,
clarinetist, recently widowed and remarried, mid-to-late thirties

DOTTY MOFFETT, Caroline's friend, early thirties

THE MOON

THE BUS

EMMIE THIBODEAUX,
Caroline's only daughter, sixteen to seventeen years old

JACKIE THIBODEAUX, Caroline's son, ten years old

JOE THIBODEAUX, Caroline's son, eight years old

MR. STOPNICK, Rose Stopnick Gellman's father, mid-seventies

SETTING

The play takes place in Lake Charles, Louisiana,
November–December 1963

1.
WASHER/DRYER

Caroline, a maid, in the basement of the Gellmans' house. She's doing the laundry, sorting the clothes.

CAROLINE

Nothing ever happen under ground
in Louisiana
cause they ain't no under ground
in Louisiana.
There is only
under water.

(Caroline opens the lid of the Washing Machine, and begins to load it with clothes.)

THE WASHING MACHINE

Consequences unforeseen.
Consequences unforeseen.
Put your faith and clothes in me,
a brand-new Nineteen-Sixty-Three
seven-cycle wash machine.

(Caroline switches the Washing Machine on.)

CAROLINE

Sixteen feet below sea level!
Torn tween the Devil
and the muddy brown sea.
Sixteen soggy feet below
the Gulf of Mexico.

(She switches on the Radio.)

THE RADIO (a trio of women)

Tough and dreary and all dishevel,
sixteen feet below sea level.
Baby,
gonna drown.
All day long
you wear a frown.
Dressed in white and
feelin low,
talkin to washer and the
radio!
Doin laundry, full of woe,
neath the Gulf of Mexico.
Sixteen feet
sixteen feet
sixteen feet beneath the sea!
Sixteen feet
sixteen feet
sixteen feet beneath the—

CAROLINE

Nothing happens under ground
in Louisiana. Cept in this house,
cept here, cept here:
At nine-thirteen Saint Anthony Street

in Lake Charles Louisiana:
This house got
a basement.

THE WASHING MACHINE

This house got
a basement.
True.
No other house round here gots one.
This one
this one
this one
do.

CAROLINE

Ain't very deep for a basement but still
it planted in the swampy soil,
sunk in the mud and the marsh and the mire,
down with the snakes and the snails and the bracken,
root to the bayou,
root to the ooze . . .

THE RADIO

. . . singing them sediment topsoil blues,
alluvial delta-silt saltwater ooze.

THE WASHING MACHINE

Hum hum hum hum
round and round I agitates
while them what does the clothes awaits,
they contemplates and speculates,
in the peace my one-horsepower
lectric motor's hum creates:

THE RADIO AND THE WASHING MACHINE

What shall be? What lies in store
in Nineteen-Sixty-Three? or -Four?

(Noah, a little boy, stands at the entrance to the basement.)

NOAH

Every day she stands between
the radio and the washing machine:
Caroline, our maid.
All day long I've been gone
at school. When I get home, they're on!
Washing machine and radio!
Down the basement steps I go!
Caroline our maid!
Caroline our maid!
Caroline! Caroline! Caroline
the President of the United States!
Caroline who's always mad,
Caroline who runs everything,
Caroline who's stronger than my dad.
In our basement, where she'll let
me light her daily cigarette.

(Caroline hands Noah one cigarette and a book of matches.)

CAROLINE

Light me up.

(Noah puts the cigarette in his mouth and lights it.)

CAROLINE

(Severely:)
Don't suck in!

(She takes the cigarette from him.)

CAROLINE

Shouldn't let you do that. Boy
when you grow up don't smoke these things.

14

NOAH

Blow me smoke rings, smoke rings smoke rings!

CAROLINE

Not today, I got to work.

NOAH

Caroline never tells me so but
I know Daddy mustn't know.
A secret her and me can share:
Our daily cigarette . . .

CAROLINE

Now muse yourself,
I got no use for you.
This basement too darn hot for two.

(Noah leaves.)

THE WASHING MACHINE

Hum hum hum hum.
Smoke you daily cigarette.

CAROLINE

Only ever smoke but one.

(A timer bell rings!)

THE WASHING MACHINE

Washin finish! Sweet and wet!
And cool! My daily task is done!

THE RADIO

Time's come to perspire!
Turn on the electric dryer!
Sucking moisture out the air,

melt the hairspray in your hair!
Turn it on, turn on despair!

THE DRYER

Caroline! Caroline!
Crank my little timer bell!

THE RADIO
Caroline! Mercy me!
Thirty-nine and divorcee!
(Mm-mm-mm.)
How on earth she gonna thrive,
when her life bury her alive?
Oh-oh-oh,
well it ain't no mystery, she
took a wrong step,
took a wrong step,
took a wrong step,
slip and fell!
Downward bound,
under ground,
found her sinful self in hell,   THE DRYER
found her sinful self in hell.   Found your sinful self in hell.
                                        And the Pit of your abasement
                                        looks a bit like this old
                                            basement:
                                        Time has come,
Time's come!   Time has come,
Time's come!   time has come,
                                        turn on the dryer!
                                        Roasty, toasty, lectric fire!
Down in hell . . .   Making my groans, making
                                            my moans,
Down in hell . . .   shivering rumbling basemental
                                            tones,
                                        cooking the meat

16

TONY KUSHNER

THE DRYER *(continued)*
right off your bones!
Laundry mine now!
You know the story:
let's make this basement
a purgatory.
Time has come
time has come
time has come to suffer heat!

CAROLINE

I got four kids.
Four kids.
Four kids.
I got divorce!
I had to—
Four kids!
Had to
get divorce!
Been twenty-two years of cleaning.
For all them years I worked and prayed.
Every day I doing laundry,
thirty-nine and still a maid.
In Nineteen-Sixty-Three!
I thought for sure by now I be
better off than this!
Thirty-nine year old!
Should be somewhere
being kiss
by Nat
King
Cole.
It Nineteen-Sixty-Three and I
wish every afternoon I die.
Cook and clean and mind that boy,
doing housework doing laundry

17

sixteen feet below the sea.
Thought for sure by now I be . . .
Someplace cooler, someplace high,
someplace where there's something dry
don't come from no lectric dryer.
Doing something finer,
something not as meek,
as getting hit
and turning cheek;
hit! and turn the other cheek.
Hit! and turn the other cheek,
doing laundry under ground
for thirty dollars every week.
Thirty dollars every week.
And I am mean and I am tough but . . .

THE WASHING MACHINE, THE DRYER AND CAROLINE
Thirty dollars ain't enough.
Thirty dollars ain't enough.

CAROLINE
Nothing happen under ground
in Louisiana.
Cause there is no under ground
in Louisiana.
There is only
under water.

2.

CABBAGE

It's the end of the work day. Caroline is finishing the laundry. Stuart Gellman and his new wife, Rose Stopnick Gellman (Noah's father and stepmother), come home from working and shopping. Noah hides in his room. Outside the house, Noah's paternal grandparents. It is twilight. Fireflies, mosquitoes, frogs and crickets.

ROSE

Caroline, there's extra food:
Sweet stuffed cabbage, cooked with brisket.
It's nutritious! Iron! Vegetables!
Bring it to your kids.

CAROLINE

I can't use none, Mrs. Gellman,
my kids don't like it,
turn they noses up.
The smell.

(The Dryer dings.)

GRANDMA GELLMAN

(Outside, to Noah:)
Your mother smoked too many cigarettes.

NOAH

(In his room:)
My father is a clarinet.

GRANDPA GELLMAN

(Outside:)
You mean he plays a clarinet.

NOAH

I mean he plays the clarinet.
My mama was a sad bassoon:
they played duets.

GRANDPA GELLMAN

She smoked those packs of cigarettes.

ROSE

Tell them cabbage is good for them!
Make them eat what's good for them!
They'll get used to the smell. I did.
Reminds me of home, a northern smell,
takes me back to
Ocean Parkway!
They'll learn to love cabbage.
I did! I did! Cabbage boiled, iron beets,
it makes them strong,
children should be strong, and BIG!
Big strong children—
(Calling:)
Noah! Noah!
He's so shy—
his mother was shy—

TONY KUSHNER

a hug could break him!
(Calling:)
Noah darling!

(Caroline ignores this, folding hot clothes from the Dryer.)

GRANDPA GELLMAN

Pack after pack of cigarettes,
we warned her they'd harm her,
she wouldn't listen.
They killed her, she's dead,
they killed her she died.

(Noah, joining Caroline in the basement, helps her fold a bedsheet.)

CAROLINE

Cancer get people when they poison sick and angry;
or it just get them cause it get them, no reason.
Took my momma same as yours.
God make cancer Noah
like he make the whole world,
you and me and this wash machine.
When cancer eat people Noah
it God eating them;
God sometimes eat people, like a wolf.
He make this whole world as a test.
Cancer was your momma's test,
and her death is your test, you been tested too.

NOAH

Did God make the dryer?

CAROLINE

No, the Devil made the dryer.
Everything else, God made.

21

NOAH

Everything else, God made!

(Noah leaves the basement.)

STUART

(In his practice room:)
There is no God, Noah,
we don't believe in God.
In all that corny stuff.
We're scientific people!
Space is infinite and empty and cold,
people are descended from apes, actually
and usually act worse than apes,
and a boy your age should sleep without a light on,
and your mother is dead
and there is no God.

GRANDMA AND GRANDPA GELLMAN

In Nineteen-Sixty-Three
our widowed son
a tragedy tragedy
married a friend
from New York City
a pity, a pity.

STUART

Wonderful things
come to an end.
Marry a friend.
Make a new start.

GRANDMA AND GRANDPA GELLMAN

Rose Stopnick can cook.
Rose Stopnick is lovely.

Rose Stopnick doesn't smoke.
Or play the bassoon.

CAROLINE

I'm going home, Mrs. Gellman,
I done wash the clothes.

ROSE

Please, call me Rose.

CAROLINE

I put up the shrimps,
I wash the floor upstairs,
I dusted the World Book Encyclopedia,
I ironed the linens . . .

ROSE

And please take some cabbage
home to your kids.

CAROLINE

Don't like the smell. Night, Mrs. Gellman.

(Caroline leaves, stands by a bus stop outside.)

NOAH AND GRANDMA AND GRANDPA GELLMAN

Rose Stopnick can cook.

NOAH

Rose Stopnick is nice to me.

STUART

Make a new start. Make a new start.

(Rose is in the basement; she has found coins in the bleach cup.)

ROSE

(Calling:)
Noah darling! Look!
You left change in your pants pockets again!

NOAH AND GRANDMA AND GRANDPA GELLMAN
Rose Stopnick doesn't smoke.

STUART
Marry a friend, make a new start . . .

NOAH
I hate her
I hate her
with all my heart.

3.
LONG DISTANCE

Rose is on the phone to her father in New York City.

ROSE

Hello Pa!
It's long distance,
it's your brand-new southern daughter,
it's Rose!
Oh everything's fine here,
I suppose.
How's the Hudson River?
I'm fine, just fine, I'm learning the lingo:
Magnolia, camellia, azalea, y'all.
The temple—get this—has Sunday night bingo—
just like the goyim.
Oy.
A long-distance call!
So much to tell. The boy still hates me.
(I really shouldn't be talking so loud.)
He leaves money in his pockets,

and that really grates me,
I tell him and tell him it's not allowed,
just shucking your laundry—
you hear that? "Shuck!"
I'm a southerner already—onto the floor;
take the money out first,
God knows we're not poor,
but show respect for your father.
He worked hard for that buck—
well, no, not a whole buck, he's a boy,
but loose change. Quarters. Those add up.
The Negro maid, she's making bupkes,
how does that look, leaving change in his pockets?
Indifferent to money,
the kid's a little funny,
spoiled and quiet—sad, I guess.
I'm on a diet. I bought a new dress.
Stu's giving lessons, playing, doing fine:
the work is steady.
He still misses Betty.
I don't mind.
I miss her too.
She was my best friend.
I miss the city.
I miss the old crowd. What?
Because we haven't got—
We *can't* give her a raise!
Pa!
We aren't rich, we're just plain folk,
we've only got bupkes ourselves—
we're broke.
Typical you obsess about the maid
while your daughter's miserable.
No, not miserable, I never said—
Well, it's not what I meant.
I'm just not . . .

Just not . . .
A hundred percent.
It's very hot, and very damp,
and out in the backyard there's a little swamp.
Full of noisy frogs. Last night I cried.
I miss you, Pa.
I miss the Upper West Side.

4.

MOON CHANGE

Out on the street, on the curb, Caroline and Dotty Moffett, another maid, are waiting for the bus.

DOTTY

Evening Caroline.

CAROLINE

Same to you.

DOTTY

How you feelin,
how you been?
Warmish for November.
(Little pause.)
Gettin dark early, huh?
Bus better not be late.
Mrs. Griffin lettin me off early these days, on account of night
    school.
She like havin a maid goin to college. Make her feel sort of fancy.

(Little pause.)
I say, it warmish for November.
(Little pause.)
Listen to them frogs,
expecting the moon.
I don't hardly ever take the bus now,
I got a boyfriend, he gots a car.
We never get to talk no more.

CAROLINE

Knees hurt,
wore out,
same as yesterday,
same tomorrow,
too tired to talk.

DOTTY

How Noah doing?

CAROLINE

Ain't my job to mind that boy.
I don't know how Noah do.
Ask him yourself.

DOTTY

Caroline, why you huff at me?
You never used to be that way,
all a sudden,
so unfriendly,
I never did no harm to you.

CAROLINE

I don't like the way you do.
You change.
Gal your age wearing bobby socks

and saddle shoes,
acting like I don't know what-all—

DOTTY

Everyone down to the college, everyone
wear these shoes, and I don't see
that you got call to—you the one that change!
You change!

CAROLINE

Plaid skirts, flip hair,
you's no kid, and run with mens
and—never mind. Drinking too.
And smoking cigarettes, and I don't know what-all.

DOTTY

Uh-oh you's getting pinched and pruney
like them ladies at your church,
think they's come at God's suggestion,
judging this one, judging that one.
Fore you got yourself divorce;
fore I told you I's going to night school;
for all that you wasn't hateful;
now you got all grim and gospel.
Sorry you is sick and shame.
Sorry you drinking misery tea.
Sorry your life ain't what it should be.
Don't see why you think it proper
to take it out on me.

CAROLINE

Seeing as how you ain't never seen
the inside of a church,
I don't think you got perspective
on what the gospel is,
Dotty Moffett, high and mighty,

goin to college every night,
leastest thing that they could teach you
is not to talk on what you's wholly
completely abysmally
ignorant of.

(Little pause with frogs singing.)

DOTTY

Where's the moon? Should be here.
Frogs is asking after it.
Gibbous moon tonight and it be
warmish for November.
Gibbous moon tonight.

THE MOON

(Offstage:)
Moon change.

DOTTY

You seen on the TV?

CAROLINE

Ain't got a TV.

DOTTY

That old copper statue?
By the courthouse downtown?
"Honorin the brave Confed'rate Soldier,
The South's Defender," the Civil War . . .
Ain't there no more,
it ain't there no more.

CAROLINE

Well where is it?

DOTTY

Last evening,
somebody heist the hateful thing,
unscrewed it,
carried it away.

CAROLINE

Now who go and do a thing like that?

DOTTY

No witness,
don't got no one's name.

Don't know who to blame.
Standin there one hundred year,
now that statue, he just disappear.
Things change everywhere, even here.

CAROLINE

It just mean trouble,
it just mean trouble on the
way,
Don't want to hear that . . .

(Pause. Dotty takes out a pack of cigarettes, offers one to Caroline. The Moon rises.)

DOTTY

Want a smoke, Miz Piety and Rectitude?

THE MOON

Moon change, moon change,
glowing bright, light up the night,
make your dress of spotless white
turn to purple, turn to gleam . . .
Cool and dry,
free and high,
miles free from basement steam.
Change come fast and change come slow
but change come, Caroline Thibodeaux.

CAROLINE

I'm wearin white hose,
my knees ain't on display,

Tony Kushner

I wears a white dress,
they like they maids that way,
Don't want em dressed for play.
I put all that away,
that's all I got to say.

DOTTY

Once you was quick,
and once you was bright;
now it seem you come to
    some confusion,

You wait forever

you losin courage, you losin
    light,

Fore that damn bus come.
My kids should be in bed.
I'm waitin here instead.
Moon gone change and change
again fore that damn bus take me home . . .

lost your old shine,
lost Caroline.

THE MOON

(With Caroline and Dotty below:)
Moon change, moon change,
glowing bright, light up the night,
make your dress of spotless white
turn to purple, turn to gleam . . .
Cool and dry,
free and high,
miles free from basement steam.
Change come fast and change come slow
but change come, Caroline Thibodeaux.

CAROLINE

Come on.

I got to get home.

It been a rough day.

DOTTY

And everyone changin their
    tune,

like the frogs, and the world,
    and the moon,

and the sky go from cloudy to
    clear.

CAROLINE (*continued*)
I put all that away.

DOTTY (*continued*)
Times change, Caroline, even
    here.

Nothing ever changes
    under ground in Louisiana.

(*The Bus arrives. He sings in a terrible voice of apocalypse:*)

THE BUS

The earth,
the earth has bled!
Woe-singing wind down the neighborhood.
He is gone now! Gone for good!
Oh-oh-oh,
gone for good!
Deluge flood ice water rise.
Tear your hair your clothes
your eyes.
Sisters, shed
tears of blood.
The earth has bled!
Now come the flood.
Apologies for being late,
making everybody wait.
Tonight the moon illuminate
more than just
a city bus:
I am the Orphan Ship of State!
Drifting! Driverless!
Moving slow
neath my awful freight of woe.
The earth,
the earth has bled.
The president
Oh blight November winter night
the president is dead.

(Little pause with frogs, which get louder.)

CAROLINE AND DOTTY

That can't be.

THE BUS

Some man kill him.
Dead in Dallas.

(Inside the house, Rose is holding the bleach cup.)

ROSE

Noah darling look
I found change
in your pants pockets again.

(Outside:)

THE BUS

News come slow here,
change come slow,
light gone out now, darkness come
Step on board;
time for departing . . .

(Inside the house:)

ROSE

Noah please come here . . .

(Outside:)

THE BUS

Into the nighttime,
toward what lies ahead.

*(Caroline and Dotty board the bus, which drives away.
Inside:)*

ROSE

I need to speak to you!

(Noah goes to Rose.)

ROSE

Why do you leave
change in your pockets?
Especially when I have asked you not to?

NOAH

I forget.

ROSE

You've got to remember!
Look! In the bleach cup,
it's more than a dollar!
Think of the things you can buy
for a dollar,
think of what Caroline thinks
in this basement,
working all day in this horrible basement.

NOAH

Caroline likes it, the basement, it's hers . . .

ROSE

Working for peanuts
and . . . *likes* it?
I doubt that!
Don't be a baby!
She's poor!

NOAH

She is not!

ROSE

Oh Noah, of course she is.
She's poor, it's embarrassing
to have her find money
just left in the laundry:
think of the things she could do with these quarters,
these nickels and pennies—

NOAH

Caroline is king
and Caroline is queen
and Caroline is stronger than my dad;
it isn't true,
she doesn't hate it,
she's a lot stronger, stronger than you.

*(Noah runs back to his room.
Outside:)*

THE MOON

Inside, outside,
this ol world change with the tide.
Outside tears and disarray!
Inside children disobey.
Change come slow, come right away!

(Inside, Rose has followed Noah to his room.)

ROSE

From now on,
Noah darling,
a new rule:
take your money out of your pockets

before you put your pants in the hamper
or else
Caroline can keep any change that she finds.
Caroline can keep any change that she finds.
You've got to get it,
you've got to learn.
Money's important,
a cause for concern.
No matter how much money gets left in
from now on it belongs to Caroline.
It's hers. I'm going to tell her.
It's hers.
(A beat.)
You got it?
(A beat.)
Noah?

(Little pause.)

NOAH

It's hers.

ROSE

That's great!
In time you'll appreciate
how I taught you how to care:
and really, darling, I think it's fair.
It's not what you're used to, but
things change.
Things change.

*(During the above, Grandma and Grandpa Gellman arrive at the house. They ring the bell.
Inside:)*

ROSE

There's the door!

NOAH

Things change.

THE MOON

Moon change.

ROSE

I wonder who'd be visiting so close to dinner?

(Outside:)

GRANDMA AND GRANDPA GELLMAN

JFK, JFK,
beat the Russians, saved the day,
stopped the Jew-haters and their bomb,
stopped their nuclear pogrom.
Dedicated to undo
American anti-Semites too!
Friend to the colored, friend to the Jew.
"Ask not what your country
can do for you!"

(Dotty appears; she is elsewhere, on board the bus:)

DOTTY

JFK, JFK,
swore to help black folk some day.
Sure he was a little slow,
getting round to doing so,
but he swore it and I know
he was set to help our cause,
meant to pass some proper laws.

DOTTY AND GRANDMA AND GRANDPA GELLMAN

Toleration for all men!
We shall not see his like again.
He is gone now, JFK . . .

DOTTY

Our almost-friend is gone away.

(Dotty vanishes.
Rose opens the front door. The elder Gellmans are standing there.)

NOAH

Dimes and quarters
under water . . .

NOAH AND THE MOON

. . . where the moon can't send her beams.

THE MOON

Moon change
moon change . . .

NOAH

Bedtime then . . .

NOAH AND THE MOON

. . . it's time for dreams.

5.

DUETS

Caroline is at home on her porch, in the dark, waiting, listening to the radio.

THE RADIO

No one waitin to warm the dark,
no one hopin that I'll wear red,
no one wantin to spark my spark,
no one needin to share my bed . . .

(Caroline's daughter Emmie arrives, on foot, and climbs the three steps to the porch.)

THE RADIO	CAROLINE
Nobody's arm to cradle my head,	Don't break promises, Emmie,
to talk about news, talk about views,	do like you say you do.
talk about change,	Don't give yourself options.
bout the president dead,	Most folks lives without em.

THE RADIO *(continued)*
bout how the day went,
or how time flown,
or life been spent,
or I'm all alone . . .

CAROLINE *(continued)*
Most folks does without.

EMMIE
Lost track of the time, Mama,
sorry, Aunt Claudia
say she'd mind the children,
say she don't mind minding
  them.
Sorry, Mama, I was out,
being shiftless, having fun.

CAROLINE
What kind of fun?

(Emmie switches the dial on the Radio to a livelier station:)

EMMIE AND THE RADIO
You remember fun, Mama;
out at the parking lot,
longside the A&W,
buncha us talking,
dancing to the radio.

CAROLINE
The president's dead.

EMMIE AND THE RADIO
I know, the radio
play music anyway!
Just some old white man
sent Larry off to Vietnam.
Sorry he dead.
I ain't killed him.

CAROLINE
I'm too tired to fight.
You don't do me right.

I can't do with no daughters
shiftless as you.

EMMIE AND THE RADIO
Just some old white man
don't care about the black man . . .

CAROLINE
Emmie Thibodeaux! Since when you say "black man"?
Say colored or Negro, like you was raised up to.

EMMIE AND THE RADIO
Say he do stuff *for* us,
get our vote, he just ignore us,
same old story, Mama, same tired old lie.
If you got to do it Mama go ahead and cry.
I ain't got no tears to shed
for no dead white guy.

(Caroline switches the Radio back to her station:)

THE RADIO
Free, free, lonesome and free!

No one pacin the floor
for me.
Flower don't need no
honeybee.
If free mean misery, that's
what I be.
Ain't nobody's baby,
ain't property,
got nothing I own
cept being alone
free and lonely . . .

CAROLINE
Go on and get yourself to bed,
girl,
whoever put a mouth like that
on you?
I know *I* didn't do it, and God
didn't do it,
and somedays I don't know
what I'm gonna do . . .

EMMIE
How your knees today?

CAROLINE

They fine, go on asleep.
Don't wake up the baby,
say prayers for us all,
give your mama a kiss,
pologize to God for being such a unholy priss,
and a caution and a sass
fore your mama whups your . . .

EMMIE

Night Mama!
Night God!
Night radio!
Night cheap beautiful music!
Night frogs in autumn,
night unseasonable frogs!
Night barking dogs
and mice-hunting cats
and cicadas in the pecan trees
and everything that dies
when winter comes!
Night lightning bugs!
Good night!

*(Emmie kisses Caroline and goes inside the house.
Noah at home in bed:)*

NOAH

President Caroline!
President Caroline Thibodeaux!

CAROLINE

Right here, right here.

NOAH

What're you gonna do now

44

that President Kennedy's dead?
Now you're the only President
in the United States!

CAROLINE

Gonna pass me a law
that night last longer.
Gonna pass me a law
Larry come home from Vietnam,
wherever that is.
Gonna pass me a law
no woman can be my age
and not know enough
to read a map.
Gonna pass me a law
that my heathen daughter
don't never get hurt
nor learn how to mind me,
nor learn how to mind
nobody cept herself.
Gonna pass me a law
say Nat King Cole
gotta come over my house
come over my house
come over every night
and stroke my soul.

NOAH

Wish me good night?

CAROLINE

That not my job.

NOAH

How come?
(Little pause.)

How come you're so sad
and angry all the time?

CAROLINE

That ain't your business, it just ain't your business.
You's a nosey child.
(Little pause.)
How come you like me, I ain't never nice to you.

NOAH

That isn't true! The cigarette!

CAROLINE

Right. The cigarette.

NOAH

My mama liked you!
I do too!
You're implacable,
indestructible, Mama said.
I'm always sad.
I like it that you're always mad.
And I can tell you like me too.
At least I think you do.

CAROLINE

Noah, go to sleep.
stop botherin the night.
All day I mind you, wash your things,
and it ain't right
in the nighttime, my own time,
I still think about you—
I gots to think about rent overdue,
cause last week twice
I bought ground chuck
and for once I didn't stuff it

full of two-day-old bread;
I fed my kids meat
stead of meat-flavored bread,
twice in one week.
Now rent overdue,
and Jackie got bad teeth, need the dentist,
spectacles too. And everyone need clothes,
they growing up rough.
And Larry need a package with cookies and stuff.
And Emmie want a TV, she want everything,
and Joe want candy, want a rat-fink ring.
And I want the night to stay
nighttime forever
so I can sit smoking here, so I never
have to get up, go to work, be polite.
Go on to bed, Noah.
Stop botherin the night.

6.

THE BLEACH CUP

Rose and Caroline in the basement.

ROSE

Noah has a problem!
A problem with money!
A problem with change,
loose change in his pockets!
He's forever leaving it, leaving it, leaving it,
maybe it's a problem with
hanging on to things,
maybe an expression,
a subconscious expression
of losing what is valuable,
you know, his mother,
maybe it's *change*,
he has learned to hate change!
I bet that's it, just call me Sigmund Freud,
don't you think I'm right, Caroline?
Noah hates change, it's an association,

I bet that that's . . .
Do your kids do things like that?
I bet they mind their money.

CAROLINE

Yes Mrs. Gellman, they good about money.

ROSE

We have to
teach Noah
we have to teach Noah
to mind his money;
to handle change!
So listen, I need you to help me to teach him.
From now on if you find
change in his pockets,
when you do the washing,
just keep it, just keep it,
if he leaves it, it's yours.

CAROLINE

I always find moneys
he leave in his pocket,
pennies and nickels.
They go in the bleach cup.
I gives his money back to him.
I don't wanna take pennies from a baby.
Give him a whupping,
stop giving him money . . .

ROSE

(Aside:)
I hope she's not offended!
I hope this is the right thing!
Oh brother this is embarrassing!
(To Caroline:)

I know, but from now on,
you keep it; I'm sure
you can probably use it.
And Noah must learn to mind it,
or lose it.
It'll be like a raise!
Like Noah pays
a share of your salary
for the cooking and cleaning,
you take such good care of us,
and—
(Aside:)
Other people's maids
are so much nicer!
She never smiles,
it'd be wrong to fire her, but
how on earth did you stand it, Betty?
Jesus, lady, smile already!
(To Caroline:)
He needs to learn consequences.
I don't believe in whupping kids.
Please, Caroline, keep the change.

*(Rose leaves the basement.
Noah and his father in Stuart's practice room:)*

STUART

Noah, you are nine years old.

NOAH

No I'm not I'm eight.

STUART

Eight? Only eight?
But you're in fourth grade now.

NOAH

No, I'm in third.

STUART

Really, you're sure?
Isn't that weird.
It's like a whole year, just . . .
I don't know, just disappeared.
I have to get back to the clarinet.
Practice the cello.

NOAH

I gave up the cello, Dad.

STUART

Oh right. You did.
I remember. You're a funny kid.
Your mother loved the cello.

NOAH

Can I go?

STUART

It's time that you should demonstrate
more responsibility.
Help Rose with groceries,
that kind of thing.
In return I'm giving you
a dollar fifty every week
allowance. You can use it as you like but I—

NOAH

Buy buy
buy buy buy!

STUART

—I hope you'll save it
till you're older
buy yourself
a chemistry set.

NOAH

Bubblegum cigarettes
sea monkeys
comic books
Barbie doll dresses on the sly!
Buy buy
buy buy buy.

STUART

That's what I wanted back when I
was a boy,
a great big shiny chemistry set.

CAROLINE

There's almost a dollar
some weeks in the bleach cup.
My kids could go down to the
    dime store and get
the shiny junk they make to
    catch a kid's eye.
And what they sees and
    what they wants
they could buy.

STUART

Stuff I can't buy em now,
always in the lurch.
Some weeks I could even
    tithe at Church.

A great big shiny chemistry set!
With test tubes, a spirit lamp,
powders, and flame.

Do you want a chemistry set?

NOAH

No.

STUART

Oh. Well, that's a shame.
It's your money Noah, so please
keep in mind . . .

ROSE

Caroline keeps what Caroline finds.

NOAH

That night I leave a dime and a nickel
in my pants pocket
to see what will happen;
Caroline finds them.

CAROLINE

They go in the bleach cup.

NOAH
They sit there all week,
fifteen cents, fifteen cents,
five jawbreakers,
a big bag of red-hots,
a *Daredevil* comic book,
fifteen cents!

CAROLINE
They sit there all week.
Fifteen cents, fifteen cents,
a bag full of sugary things
stain the mouth orange
stain the teeth green
that upset the stomach . . .
A grown woman got no business
taking pennies from a baby.

(Caroline removes the change from the bleach cup and puts it in her pocket.)

NOAH

Caroline took my money home!
My money home in her pocketbook!
I leave a quarter to see what will happen.

CAROLINE

Quarter in the bleach cup, take it home.

NOAH

I leave two more quarters. To see what she'll do.

CAROLINE

Quarters in the bleach cup, take them home.

NOAH

Then I left a dollar bill
in my pocket
by mistake.

CAROLINE

He left a dollar in his pocket.
A dollar bill.

(Caroline hands the dollar to Noah.)

CAROLINE

(Angry!)
Left this dollar
in your pocket!
Mind your money!
Lucky for you I didn't take it.

NOAH

Can I light your cigarette?

CAROLINE

No you can't! Now go on get!
You ain't lighting no more cigarettes
never again and if I catch you
playing with matches I tell your mama.

NOAH

My mama's dead!

CAROLINE

You hear what I said?!
Spend your money on them funny books
and don't try out your dirty looks!
Take your dollar, get upstairs!
Out my basement!

NOAH

(To Caroline:)
I don't want a cigarette! Who cares!
(Little pause.)
I leave another quarter.

CAROLINE

I leave it in the bleach cup.

NOAH

I leave another quarter.

CAROLINE

Two quarters in the bleach cup,
I leave em be.

NOAH

I leave another quarter.
Seventy-five cents.

CAROLINE

And I am mean and I am tough
but thirty dollars ain't enough.
Thirty dollars and
seventy-five cents . . .

(Caroline takes the money out of the bleach cup and puts it in her purse.)

NOAH

Caroline takes my money home!
Now I know what they talk about
at the Thibodeaux house, at suppertime.
Before it was a mystery.
Now they count my quarters and
they talk about me!

(Caroline at her house; calls Emmie, Jackie and Joe to the front porch.)

CAROLINE

Emmie!

EMMIE

Mama?

CAROLINE

Jackie!

JACKIE

Yes'm?

CAROLINE

You too, Joe.

JOE

We done somethin bad?

CAROLINE

Hold your hand out.
Go on, close your eyes.

(They do as they're told. Caroline puts a quarter into each hand.)

CAROLINE

Open sesame!
Tell me what you see!
Somethin silver shiny all your own now,
all your own.

EMMIE, JACKIE AND JOE

All our own!

(The kids stare at the quarters and then watch as Caroline goes inside the house.)

JACKIE

It's a quarter.

JOE

Mama ain't got money.
(Calling, into the house:)
Hey MAMA! Where'd this money come from, you—

EMMIE

(Interrupting him on "money":)
Leave her be! Don't get her goin.

JACKIE

But it's a—

EMMIE

If she wanted to tell she'd of told you. Know what happens to children who snoop?

JOE

What?

EMMIE

There was this one boy, he asked his mama one too many
questions and he died. He *died*.

JOE

Aw shut up.

EMMIE

He did!

JACKIE

For true?

EMMIE

For true.
Once upon a time in a shack by the lake
live a boy and his mama so broke they break.
Ugliest child that you ever saw,
name Roosevelt Petrucius
Coleslaw!

Roosevelt Petrucius
Coleslaw!
Didn't have a penny.
No he didn't have any.
So he asked his ma,
Old Lady Coleslaw!
"Ma I'm broke
and
Ma I'm glum!"
And Glory Hallelujah to Kingdom Come!
Ma reach in her pockets . . .

EMMIE, JACKIE AND JOE

. . . and she give him some!

EMMIE

"Look here Roosevelt, see here Ro!
I got a penny!"

JACKIE AND JOE

"NO, MAMA, NO!"

EMMIE

"I got a nickel."

JACKIE AND JOE

"Won't buy a pickle!
THAT'S NO GO,
you WAY TOO SLOW!"

EMMIE

"I got a dime."

JACKIE AND JOE

"Now that's a crime!"

EMMIE

"How bout a quarter?"

JACKIE AND JOE

"Well *that's* a starter . . ."

EMMIE

"I got two!"

JACKIE AND JOE

"MAMA I LOVE YOU!"

EMMIE

"Got three quarters
to be spent!"

JACKIE AND JOE

"Pretty Mama Coleslaw!
Seventy-five cent!"

NOAH

Caroline shows each silver quarter
to her kids—
she's a divorcee!
"Thank God we can eat now
thanks to poor crazy Noah,
who's just a stoopnagle
can't hang on to a quarter!"
But at least now at supper
they talk about me.

EMMIE, JACKIE AND JOE

Sweet old Missus Coleslaw,
she say, "Roosevelt Roosevelt have you a time,
spend a little money at the five and dime!"

JACKIE AND JOE

But Roosevelt Petrucius Coleslaw,
he born dumb, he say,
"Mama oh Mama where this change come from?
Mama oh Mama where this change come from?"

EMMIE

Mama went wild,
"I earnt it child!"

EMMIE, JACKIE AND JOE

Then she whacked him and she smacked him

upside his head,
but she hit too hard and the child dropped dead!

JACKIE

And he sprouted wings and he flew up to heaven,
and heaven look like the 7-11!

JOE

And all the stars of heaven they was pennies and dimes:

EMMIE

Red-hot!

JACKIE

Sweet-tart!

EMMIE, JACKIE AND JOE

Lemons and limes!

EMMIE

Moon pie, food dye, Tootsie-pop!

JACKIE AND JOE

Pop gun, squirt gun, sticky bun,
Silly-putty, Nutty-butter, sixty-four colors
in the Crayola pack
pack pack!

EMMIE

Bird call, slap paddle,
Tinkywinks, skip rope,
licorice, Pickup sticks!

JACKIE AND JOE

Magic tricks, Lego bricks, pirate hooks and comic books!

JACKIE, JOE AND NOAH
COMIC BOOKS!

JACKIE
Superman

JOE
Batman

JACKIE
Aquaman

JOE
and Ironman

JACKIE AND JOE
Spiderman, X-Men, Daredevil, Doctor Strange and

EMMIE
Wonder Woman! Diana!

EMMIE AND NOAH
Princess of the Amazons!
Magical lariat, golden tiara,
bulletproof bracelets, lipstick and mascara!

JOE
Stronger than anyone, six times as pretty,
An eagle brassiere with a wing on each titty!

EMMIE, JACKIE, JOE AND NOAH
Wing on each titty!
Wing on each titty!
Tittytittytittytittytittytittytittytitty!

NOAH

They talk about how my mama died
they talk about my tragedy
they wish that they could take me in
and I could live with Caroline
and Emmie Jackie Larry Joe,
Emmie Jackie Larry Joe.
Each evening I could up and go
home to be a Thibodeaux.
Emmie Jackie Larry Joe
and Noah
Noah Thibodeaux.

EMMIE, JACKIE, JOE AND NOAH

She did it, she did it,
she kill her kid!
Oh Mama, oh Mama
see what you did!
R.I.P.!

EMMIE

She found him dead, his mean old ma,
she screamed, "Roosevelt Petrucius Coleslaw!
Oh my child, my darling son,
your time on earth is gone and done,
and you are lost and gone before!"

JACKIE

But Roosevelt an angel now,
he bought out the store,
and he still got nickels and dimes galore!
His mama cry, "He's gone too soon!"
But Roosevelt is sitting longside of the moon,
and he says, "Miss Moon, will you be my Mrs.?"

THE MOON

I might, you sweet but you gotta be rich!

JACKIE, JOE AND NOAH
"I'm rich, I'm rich, will you give me kisses?"

THE MOON
I will sweet pea, indeed I shall,
I'll be your lovey little looney gal!
Cause you are sweet and you are rich!

JACKIE, JOE AND NOAH
So they went up to God and they got hitch!

THE MOON
And I will wax and I will wane,
I'll turn your brain into green moon cheese,
I'll do every first thing that I please,
I'll be your honey and I'll spend all your money
but I'll shine so bright
I'll be your delight,
and I'll grow full and I'll grow fat
and you'll say to yourself:

JACKIE, JOE AND NOAH
"Now how about that?!"
"Now how about that?!"

THE MOON
And that's the last . . .

EMMIE, JACKIE, JOE, NOAH AND THE MOON
. . . that anyone saw
of Roosevelt Petrucius Coleslaw!
He flap his wings and he flew away,
and said good-bye to heaven and to JFK,
and he's flying through space to this very day,
counting all the stars in the Milky Way.
He counts so high he's a millionaire,
and he doesn't have a care.

TONY KUSHNER

(While the kids continue their game, Caroline appears in the basement of the Gellmans' house.)

EMMIE, JACKIE, JOE, NOAH AND THE MOON	CAROLINE
Ching! Ching! Ching! Chingalinga!	And now every morning, day after day,
Ching! Ching! Ching! Chingalinga!	there's change in his pockets.
Ching! Ching! Ching! Chingalinga!	Quarters, pennies—
Ching! Ching! Ching! Chingalinga!	He's leavin them there.
A penny for Rosie and off he go!	And I am mean
A nickel, a quarter, he got some dough!	and I am tough
He rise in the skies, and look down below, and say:	but thirty dollars ain't enough.
"I'm a gonna buy me The Sky!	Thirty dollars.
Didn't have a penny yeah but now I got plenty	
so I say good-bye—	Thirty dollars.
No Mama don't cry!	
If I'm broke!	

CAROLINE

Ain't right!

EMMIE, JACKIE, JOE, NOAH AND THE MOON

If I'm glum!

CAROLINE

Ain't decent!

EMMIE, JACKIE, JOE, NOAH AND THE MOON
Glory Hallelujah to Kingdom Come!

CAROLINE
Change in his pockets just lyin there!

EMMIE, JACKIE, JOE, NOAH AND THE MOON	CAROLINE
I reach in my pockets and I find me some!	I reach in his pockets and I find me some!

CAROLINE
For free!

EMMIE, JACKIE, JOE, NOAH AND THE MOON
I'm free as the air . . ."

CAROLINE
Free as the air!

INTERMISSION

7.

IRONING

Caroline is in the basement. She is holding the bleach cup. She gives it a shake. It's full of coins; they jingle.

THE RADIO

Santa comin, Caroline!
Hark the Herald, Joy Divine!
Jingle bells driftin through the pine!
Way down South it don't snow
so you know
it's a sign!

Loose change in the laundry
ring like Santa's sleigh!
Should you leave em in the bleach cup?
Should you take them jinglin coins away?

Season's greetings, Caroline!
Take the change! Why you disincline?
Does it taste like a bitter wine?

Mistletoe hangin low—
Go on,
bend your spine!

Ain't right to take his pennies.
They ain't Santa's sleigh.
Yeah but Christmas is expensive,
you got gifts to buy and bills to pay.

So Noel, baby, auld lang syne!
You been good, baby, toed the line.
Now go on, berry's on the vine!
Jing-a-ling,
money bring
caroling,
Caroline!

THE WASHING MACHINE

Little reward.

CAROLINE

Shouldn't take it.

THE WASHING MACHINE

Little present.

CAROLINE

I don't need it.

THE WASHING MACHINE	CAROLINE AND THE RADIO
Little bit of	Pickin pockets, countin change!
Breathin room	THE RADIO
Water make the flower bloom!	Baby . . .

THE WASHING MACHINE, THE RADIO AND CAROLINE
. . . You learn to rearrange!

Tony Kushner

THE WASHING MACHINE

Little money to be spent,
little bit of supplement.

CAROLINE

Can't afford embarrassment.

THE WASHING MACHINE AND THE RADIO

Take it home.

CAROLINE

Money don't buy happiness.

THE WASHING MACHINE

Pocket change for . . .

THE WASHING MACHINE AND THE RADIO

Sayin Yes!

THE WASHING MACHINE

Little blessings, gone unless
you take em home.

CAROLINE

Little bit of grace . . .

THE WASHING MACHINE

. . . erase that frown.
You start to let your guard down . . .

THE RADIO

All changes come from small changes
come from coin janglin in the wash machine,
knock you off your routine
ways; you rattled nowadays, in the face of
silver, shiny opportunities—
you give in to memories . . .

THE WASHING MACHINE

Nineteen-Forty-Three you marry . . .

CAROLINE

Handsome boy, a navy man.
He go off to fight Japan.

THE WASHING MACHINE

You stay home . . .

CAROLINE

Give birth to Larry.
Then three years of lonely waiting.
Fearful prayers.
Anticipating.

THE WASHING MACHINE

Nineteen-Forty-Five the navy
send you home your handsome man.

THE RADIO

Life is sunny, life is gravy.

CAROLINE

Thank you Jesus, thank you navy!
He is home now, every limb
is beauty, lovely like a tree.
Falling deep in love with him.

THE RADIO

The handsome navy man!
Falling deep in love with him,
long and tall and sweet and slim.

CAROLINE AND THE RADIO

Even now your hand can summon
how his neck, his belly feel,

shoulders, what his breath was like.
Hands burn then with happy fire,
every inch of you, desire,
longing set your skin aflame.

CAROLINE

Nurse the baby.
Sing his name.

THE RADIO

Sing his name!

THE WASHING MACHINE AND THE RADIO
Back in Nineteen-Forty-Seven

CAROLINE

Ain't no work for Negro men.

THE WASHING MACHINE
You's both hanging on to heaven.

CAROLINE

Emmie come . . .

THE WASHING MACHINE AND THE RADIO
Shipyard close

CAROLINE

mmonia factory almost hire him.

THE RADIO
Only white mens in that union.

CAROLINE

He get drunk, he scared, he angry,
feeling hopeless, I suppose . . .

71

CAROLINE, OR CHANGE

THE WASHING MACHINE

He hit you.

CAROLINE

Just once.

THE WASHING MACHINE

He break your nose.

CAROLINE

Larry is a gentle baby.
Emmie fussy, never sleeps.
He gets drunk. He broke my nose.

THE RADIO

Even now your face can summon

CAROLINE

what his punch feel like, the pain.

THE RADIO

Pain is white, remember pain?
Pain is white, that is its color,
bright as sunshine.
Nighttime follow.
Bitterness you drink and swallow.

CAROLINE

God whose eye is on the sparrow,
please make Emmie go to bed.
Folk'll stare tomorrow. Jesus,
please fix up my swollen head.
Please a job so he stop drinking.
Please, he don't like digging sewers.

THE WASHING MACHINE

No one likes that diggin sewers.

CAROLINE

Please give me a mop and bucket.
Please, a white folks' house to tend.
Please some money, feed the babies,
choke his throat when he drink liquor,
make my sis help with my babies,
let him see
he mess with me
after I have spent the day
putting white folks' clothes away,
tell him God, if he ever
ever
ever hit me again . . .

THE RADIO

Larry, Emmie, Jackie, Joe.

THE WASHING MACHINE

Other men find work.

CAROLINE

He don't.

THE RADIO

Change come fast and change come slow

THE WASHING MACHINE

Other men leave drink . . .

CAROLINE

. . . he can't.

THE WASHING MACHINE

Ahead of time you're gettin old.
Care beatin down on you.
Then one day . . .

CAROLINE AND THE WASHING MACHINE

Then one day . . .

CAROLINE

One bad day . . .
He hit again

THE WASHING MACHINE

You beat him black and blue.
Then
he disappear from view . . .

CAROLINE AND THE RADIO

And even now your hand can summon

CAROLINE

what it like to beat his face in.
What his back feel like, his kiss.

THE WASHING MACHINE

Even now, your scar hand miss

CAROLINE

the handsome boy, the navy man.

CAROLINE, THE WASHING MACHINE AND THE RADIO

Sorrow bleed you.

CAROLINE

Where is he?

CAROLINE, THE WASHING MACHINE AND THE RADIO

You are sixteen sixteen sixteen
sixteen sixteen

ROSE

(Calling, offstage:)
Caroline!

CAROLINE

sixteen feet beneath the sea.

(Rose enters carrying a man's dress shirt.)

ROSE

Caroline, look at Mr. Gellman's shirt!
He must've left a quarter
in the front breast pocket.
You must've ironed over it!
Look! It's the head
of the Father of our Country!
Mr. George Washington,
seared into the fabric
like the face of Jesus
on the Shroud of Turin!
So I guess Mr. Gellman has to learn the rule:
he loses any change he leaves
and you can keep it,
just like Noah's, you can keep it,
just like Noah's—

CAROLINE

I don't want it!
I ain't some ragpick.
Ain't some jackdaw.

ROSE

Of course you're not a—

CAROLINE

I don't want your husband's money!

ROSE

Oh it's not your fault about the quarter!

CAROLINE

I got a load of laundry left
so excuse me, Mrs. Gellman.
From now on I'll check every pocket,
put the money in the bleach cup,
his and Noah's, yours as well.

ROSE

Oh I never leave my money in my pockets,
my father would've "whupped" me, smacked me, he—

CAROLINE

(Suddenly furious:)
If I find money now
I put it in the bleach cup
and you people do
whatever you want with it.
Take the damn money
Mrs. Gellman.
Stop bothering me with it.
You need anything else?
You need anything anything anything else?

ROSE

Now wait a second, lady—

CAROLINE

I got to iron now,
iron now iron now,
it cramp in here and there's no air
so please get out
so my arm can swing
with this hot iron
and not hit nobody.

THE WASHING MACHINE

Oooh child, watch yourself,
struck boss lady like a hammer!
Leave them coins up on that shelf!
Ooh, child, gone too far!

THE RADIO

Talk like that, talk like that,
you won't be a maid no more.

(Caroline irons. Rose is shocked, looks down at the shirt. They're both silent.)

THE WASHING MACHINE	THE RADIO
Please please boss lady boss lady New York lady don't don't fire me fire me can't do without do without do without money!	Talk like that, talk like that, you won't be a maid no more

ROSE

Caroline, I . . .
Never mind.
I wanted to tell you
my father is coming
for Chanukah soon.
So let's make up the guest room
when you get a second,
and also next Sunday
could you ask Dot and Emmie
to help with a party
from seven to ten?

CAROLINE

I have to ask Dotty.

ROSE

I'm just trying to help you,
you know, with the money.
It was only a game.
(Aside:)
So sue me already,
Miss Crabby Appleton!
I don't know what's eating you!
Some people, honestly!
There's oppression and misery,
and then there are people
who're just plain nasty.
(To Caroline:)
Just trying to be friendly.
Just trying to be a friend.

(Caroline nods, not looking up from the ironing.)

ROSE

Anyway the shirt's still good.
Look! Where the quarter was!
You can almost read the little writing!
LIBERTY! IN GOD WE TRUST!
You must've been ironing mighty hard,
that's why the clothes
come out so crisp.
General George Washington
would approve of you.
How're those kids?

(The Dryer bell dings!)

ROSE

Those kids of yours?

CAROLINE

Got to get the clothes out the dryer,
Mrs. Gellman.

THE DRYER

Some folks goes
to school at nights.
Some folks march
for civil rights.
Some folks prosper,
then they's those . . .

ROSE

The shirt's still good, just a little burnt.

THE DRYER

. . . pickin coins
from dirty clothes.

ROSE

Take it, or use it for cleaning or something.
See you upstairs.

(Rose leaves.)

THE DRYER

Caroline,
something else
on your mind sides
jingle bells.
You the queen of keep-at-bay
what-was-once or might-have-been.
Little change, and strange to say,
yesterday come crashin in.
Small domestic tragedies
bring strong women to their knees . . .

(Jackie and Joe appear singing "I Saw Three Ships Come Sailing." In the basement, Emmie rises up out of the laundry basket.)

EMMIE

Mama there's money
down in the laundry!
Dig for the money
down in the laundry!
Mama come home.
Jackie got a cavity,
eating that candy you always buying now,
he needs the dentist, and I need five dollars
to go to Beaumont,
to see the Live Nativity,
and Christmas is coming,
and money wanting.
Mama there's money
down in the laundry!
Dig for the money
down in the laundry!
Mama come home.

CAROLINE

The handsome boy.
The navy man.
Larry now in Vietnam . . .
. . . somewhere near China,
near Japan.

8.

THE CHANUKAH PARTY

All the Gellmans, and Rose's father, Mr. Stopnick, in the living room,
gathered around the menorah.
In the kitchen, preparing the food, Caroline, Dotty and Emmie;
Caroline and Dotty in maid's uniforms and Emmie in a Sunday dress.

THE GELLMANS AND MR. STOPNICK
Chanukah oh Chanukah,
oh Dreidel and Menorah!
We celebrate it even though
it isn't in the Torah!
Talmud barely mentions it,
the way they kept that candle lit;
sages in their colloquies
say bupkes bout the Maccabees
and how with very little fuss
they routed King Antiochus.
Antiochus! Pooh!
Who cares what all the sages say?
We celebrate it anyway!

Chanukah oh Chanukah,
from Astrakhan to Panama,
all along that isthmus,
we're celebrating Chanukah,
especially in America!

GRANDMA GELLMAN
A whole week more than Christmas!

ROSE
You may think it's December,
but Noah, dear, remember,
tonight is Kislev Twenty-Five!

THE GELLMANS AND MR. STOPNICK
And every single Jew alive,
Oy Noahleh, oy bubaleh,
oy vontzeleh oy pishkeleh,
sings happy happy Chanukah,
especially in America!
America America God shed His
    grace on thee,
where every Jew's a Maccabee
and crown'd thy good with
    brotherhood . . .

NOAH
and bade our blessings multiply: *(Lighting the first candle:)*
Mi kamocha ba-eilim Adonai?   Boruch ata adonai eloheinu
                melech ha'olam asher
Mi kamocha ne-e-dar   kidshanu b'mitzvotav
    ba-ko-desh?   vitzivanoo l'hadlich ner
No-ra t'hilot o-se fe-le,   shel Chanukah.
No-ra t'hilot o-se fe-le.
Omayn.

(Noah sneaks into the kitchen to watch the women work:)

CAROLINE

Give that liver salad a toss
and watch the goose don't let it dry.
Spoon them jars of applesauce
and put them pancakes in the fry!
If you don't fry em right away
they start turning gray.

NOAH

Know why they're fried in chicken fat?

EMMIE

To crisp em up.

CAROLINE

Now Noah, scat!
You's bothering us, you's underfoot.

NOAH

To symbolize the temple oil.

CAROLINE

Dot, don't let the gravy boil!
Noah, scoot, I got no use
for you tonight.

EMMIE

How about the goose?
Does that mean something?

NOAH

That's just food.

(Rose enters the kitchen:)

ROSE

Noah, out! It's very rude
to bother people when they're busy.
You aren't needed in here. Is he?

CAROLINE

No he ain't.

ROSE

Go on, don't pout.
Go on out, and see our friends, he
never listens!

(In the living room Mr. Stopnick is holding forth:)

MR. STOPNICK

The South is in a mighty frenzy!

ROSE

(In the kitchen:)
Time to bring the latkes out!
Noah tell them food is coming.

MR. STOPNICK

(In the living room:)
Wait and see!
The old world's ending!
Negroes marching!
Change is coming!
Down with the filthy capitalist chazzerim!

GRANDPA GELLMAN	ROSE
	(In the kitchen:)
Oh my . . .	Come and visit with Grandpa Stopnick,
	all the way from New York City!

(Rose sweeps Noah along with her into the living room.)

MR. STOPNICK

Just like we predicted back in the '30s,
all the Negroes got to do now
is stop this nonsense about nonviolence!

GRANDMA AND GRANDPA GELLMAN

Scary scary such a tsimmes!
Negroes in Louisiana
aren't like in Mississippi,
not as mad as Alabama.
Anyway is this the way
to talk on Erev Chanukah?
Let's not dwell on ugly things!
Let's thank God for the joys He brings!
Watch the colored candles melt!
Spin the dreidel for Chanukah Gelt!
Let's be merry, let's be funny!

GRANDMA GELLMAN

Noah, look!

GRANDPA GELLMAN

It's chocolate money!

GRANDMA AND GRANDPA GELLMAN

Let's wish our Negro neighbors well!

MR. STOPNICK

And may Bull Connor roast in hell!

GRANDMA AND GRANDPA GELLMAN AND MR. STOPNICK

Bull Connor! Pooh!

GRANDMA AND GRANDPA GELLMAN

But tonight let's just forget!

GRANDMA GELLMAN

Stuart! Play your clarinet!

(Stuart plays hot klezmer licks. Grandma Gellman begins to sing, sway, clap her hands. Mr. Stopnick joins her. Mr. Stopnick and Grandma Gellman dance. Rose tries to get Noah to dance; he won't. Rose dances alone. Grandpa Gellman claps his hands.
In the kitchen:)

DOTTY

What did I tell you?
That courthouse statue,
Confederate soldier?
You see the TV news last night?

EMMIE

We ain't got a TV.

DOTTY

Found the headless body
in Choo Choo Bayou,
wrapt in a flag, in the muddy Stars and Bars.

EMMIE

Anybody said
what happened to the head?

DOTTY

Can't find the head. They's agitated,
"Johnny Reb's decapitated!"
Dredged the bayou, lakefront too,
trawlers, spotlights, minesweepers—

EMMIE

Dang!

DOTTY

Oh uh *huh*. The whole shebang.
Bloodhounds bayin,
makin noise—
They say it was "hoodlums" done it.
They mean colored boys.

EMMIE

But they ain't said who—

DOTTY

Nope. Not a clue.
Tell you what: whoever did it—
Good for them!
I hope they burnt it
in a trash incinerator,
fed it to an alligator.
Ugly thing. Ugly thing!
The South's Defender.
Hey! Cracker Joe,
LEE SURRENDERED!
The thing is over, baby! Dead!
Don't cry!
And kiss that huge ugly head
good-bye.

EMMIE

Yeah. Let it be, for goodness sakes.
Heads go missin. Them's the breaks.
Stakes ain't high—

DOTTY

My eye they ain't.
They'll keep lookin.
Some of them is vexed as snakes
and trouble comin.

(A beat.)

EMMIE

And someone gone and killed that man
that crazy man who killed the president,
right on TV! Saw that picture
in the paper,
shot by a bullet,
look like it hurt.
We ain't got a TV set, not yet.
We only got a radio.

CAROLINE

OK, go!
Time to bring them pancakes out!
They dips them in the applesauces.
(To Emmie:)
Take the tray out, don't be spillin.
(To Dotty:)
Carve the goose and let's be trekkin.

(Emmie exits with a tray.
In the kitchen and the living room:)

CAROLINE

I don't want my child to hear that.
Negroes stealin white folk statues.

MR. STOPNICK

Now I say this with due respect:

MR. STOPNICK	CAROLINE
(In living room:)	*(In kitchen:)*
They got to stop looking for martyrdom	We are asking for disaster,

MR. STOPNICK *(continued)*	CAROLINE *(continued)*
Blow the bastards to kingdom come,	We'll be ruint fore this is over.
like the Wobblies used to do!	
Show these rednecks a thing or two!	

GRANDMA AND GRANDPA GELLMAN

(In the living room:)
Such a shonde such a tsimmes!
Noah look! Here come the latkes!
And golden may our blessings be!
Just like these lovely latkes we—

MR. STOPNICK

(Interrupting them:)
I been waiting since the '30s,
selling goddamn hats for Macy's,
waiting for the revolution,
for the fight against oppression,
for the worker to take over,
for the poor to rise in fury.
Now the Negro leads the way!
Comes at last the freedom day!
But this martyr business is a ruse!

(Caroline and Dotty enter with the goose and other goodies on trays.)

ROSE

Hallelujah! Here's the goose!
Papa, look we saved the pupick
just for you! The pupick, Papa!

MR. STOPNICK

Yes I know it worked just dandy
for that Indian Mister Ghandi
but with respect for Martin Luther King—

EMMIE

I think it's a Negro thing,
a southern thing,
a Christian thing.
Mister, you don't understand
how Dr. King has got things planned.

MR. STOPNICK

Oh Jews can be nonviolent too.
There's nothing meeker than a Jew!
Listen girlie, we have learned:
nonviolence will get you burned.

EMMIE

No I'm sorry that ain't so.
Listen to the radio.
What we're trying's already working!
Segregation's already dying!

MR. STOPNICK

I been on the earth a while.
Your optimism makes me smile.

Good for you you're optimistic!
But I think it ain't realistic.

ROSE

Papa, this is Emmie.
Emmie, this is Mr. Stopnick,
he—

EMMIE

I'd like to know how you come to feel
you know so much about what is real,
sitting safe and high and pretty,
way up North in New York City?
I'd like to know!

CAROLINE

Emmie!

EMMIE

Mama—

CAROLINE

I said quit!

EMMIE

He the one that started it!

ROSE

You know I was reading in the paper just the other day—

EMMIE

I'd like to know how
some guy just off a plane
marchin in to explain,
guess you seen it all plain
from the air?
It our
affair.
Now our resistance
start to make a difference
here come your "assistance."

MR. STOPNICK

Is that so?
Why's it so impossible to know,
white or Jew or Negro,
if the boss's boot's in your face—
what do you do? Shed a tear?
Keep lying there?
A face knows it's no footrest
regardless of religion or race!

CAROLINE

(Furious:)
CHILD YOU HEAR ME? HUSH YOUR MOUTH!
March that tray back to the kitchen.

(Emmie goes back into the kitchen, humiliated.)

MR. STOPNICK

Lady, please, since I come South,
she's my first real conversation.
Let her stay!

CAROLINE

It's past her bed.

ROSE

It's good that she's high-spirited!

CAROLINE

Yes'm. Thank you. We'll start cleaning,
in the kitchen, then go home.

(Dotty and Caroline go into the kitchen.)

DOTTY

She was doing fine out there.

CAROLINE

Dotty this ain't your affair.
(To Emmie:)
You can't talk to folk like that.

EMMIE

Talk to white folk what you mean.

CAROLINE

Lord I raised a spoiled brat.
They your boss! You ain't a queen!
Gonna get yourself knocked flat,
mouth off round white folk like that.

EMMIE

(Exploding:)
You tippy-toe till you been paid.
You the spoiled one! A maid!
I'll never be a queen, that's true,
but I'm a damn sight better'n prouder'n you!
Come on, teach me what you know!

Mama teach me what you know!
How to keep my head tucked low.
Come on, come on
teach me what you know!

(Caroline slaps Emmie, then grabs her coat and leaves the house.)

DOTTY

Watch your mouth now, little sister.
You too smart to act a fool.
Proud don't talk trash to her mother.

EMMIE

You got plans, you go to school.
What she got? Only angry, always
fussin, always shushin me.

DOTTY

Ain't seen you lackin food to eat,
Roof above, shoes on your feet.
You watch your pride ain't just conceit.
Think bein a maid what she prefer?
Go on, make things like they were.
Apologize to her.

(Emmie starts to follow her mother, then stops, and helps Dotty with the kitchen.)

MR. STOPNICK

(In the living room:)
Noah! Attention! Now comes your gift! Something handy:
Chanukah Gelt, for real, not candy!
(He takes a crisp twenty dollar bill from his wallet:)
A twenty dollar bill!

GRANDMA AND GRANDPA GELLMAN

Oh my!

MR. STOPNICK

A twenty dollar bill! And why?
Upon what should we contemplate?
Allow me please to explicate:
What's the meaning of this Gelt?

For peace sometimes, blood must be spilt.
For life, sometimes, a good man dies.
What means this money, Noah boychick?
You won't learn this in Arithmetic!

Money follows certain laws,
it's worth how much it's worth because
somewhere, something's valued less;
it's how our blessings come, I guess.
Golden, shiny, but never pure.
Think from whence your riches stem.
Think of someone who is poor:
and know you stole this gold from them.
Especially here in the Devil's South!
You rip your gold from a starving man's mouth!

ROSE

Oh for pete's sake Dad!
Give him the money!

(*Mr. Stopnick hands the bill to Noah.*)

ROSE

Good!
Say thank you, honey.

NOAH

Thank you.

MR. STOPNICK

Noah!
Never forget!

GRANDMA GELLMAN

Stuart, play the clarinet!

(Stuart plays again. Noah is frozen, looking at the twenty.)

ROSE

Right!
A happy happy Chanukah night!
What a party, what a goose!
Fun, huh? Noah?

(Noah runs upstairs.)

ROSE

Oh what's the use?

(Outside:)

DOTTY

It's cold tonight; my feet are numb;
I'm tired waiting for a bus that won't come.

EMMIE

I hate the bus, I want my own car,
a car with a heater, want a TV set, and more;
a big old house like this one, but everything new,
where can't nobody ever
can't nobody ever
tell me what to do.
Go out when I want to . . .

ROSE

Stuart.

EMMIE

. . . when I don't, then I stay.

ROSE

Go see is Noah all right.

EMMIE

Got magical bracelets, so bullets bounce away . . .

ROSE

Tuck him in for the night.

EMMIE

In every room a TV, and my own telephone,
and I live in my house
and I live in my house
by myself, all alone.
And if I'm lonely, doesn't matter,
I think they's worse than bein' lonely—
They's people who freeze
while they wait on their knees
and they don't know for what
and they just been forgot
and I
ain't waitin no more.
You just wait forever
if you can't say what for.
The day come soon, I'll pack up the nothin I own.
And I'll live in my house, and I'll make it OK,
by myself, all alone.

(The Moon appears, vocalizing. She is a new moon, dark.)

THE MOON	EMMIE
Dona, dona . . .	All alone, all alone . . .

(Inside:)

STUART
(Starting up the stairs, then freezes; aside:)
To him I have grown as remote as Tibet.
The bigger he grows, the stranger we get.
Gone are the days of our simple duet:
his piccolo piping, my bass clarinet.
All gone, nothing left but a note of regret.   THE MOON
Never oh never oh never forget her,   Dona, dona . . .
never forget her oh never forget.

(Rose is below, watching.)

                              ROSE

Look, see Rose's husband,
Gone stiff in midair,
the heartbroke musician
who froze on the stair.
Oh Stu do you love me?
The question's unfair:
How can you be loved by
someone who's not there?

STUART
Can't go up to see him, I'll only upset
my sad little son; but I can't go down yet.
She needs from me things that I cannot provide:
conversation, support, and a heart . . . Those all died.
I'll stand here eight days till the last candle's burned,
and the guests and the maid and poor Rose have returned
to wherever they came from. Till Noah has grown,
he and I will live here, in this house, all alone,
and I'll say to him, "Noah, the moon shone so bright
when she played her bassoon that last Chanukah night.

STUART *(continued)*
Oh do you remember?
  The way that it shone?
On the house,

on the three of us here,   THE MOON

all alone . . .   Dona, dona . . .
All alone . . ."

EMMIE
And I live in my
  house,
and I'll make it
  OK,
by myself, all alone.
And Mama I'm
  sorry
I called you a maid.

9.

THE TWENTY DOLLAR BILL

In the Gellmans' house, the next day.
Stuart, Rose and Mr. Stopnick are at the breakfast table:

NOAH

The next day I go off to school.

ROSE

Noah darling study hard!
You should see his last report card, Papa,
everything Cs and Ds.

MR. STOPNICK

(Reading the paper:)
Look at this! The hypocrites!
Eulogizing, rhapsodizing!
Kennedy! Kennedy!
They hated him! They murdered him! Did him in!
And *now* . . .

(Caroline enters to start her day.)

ROSE

Good morning Caroline.

(Noah is now at school.)

NOAH

All day long I sit at school,
drifting dreaming in the classroom,
inattentive cause I'm BORED!

ROSE, STUART AND MR. STOPNICK

Study Noah study hard!

(The Gellmans and Mr. Stopnick disappear.)

NOAH

Drawing doodles, Maccabees,
bumblebees, Christmas trees
and all the toys I plan to buy with . . .
Buy with . . .
Buy with . . .

(In the basement, Caroline with a laundry basket.
She takes a twenty dollar bill out of Noah's pants pocket. Caroline
stares at the twenty. She pockets it.
Grandma and Grandpa Gellman appear to Noah as the classroom
clock:)

GRANDMA AND GRANDPA GELLMAN

Suddenly he sits up straight!
SUDDENLY HE CAN CONCENTRATE!
Suddenly open go the eyes!

NOAH

Suddenly I realize:

GRANDMA AND GRANDPA GELLMAN

A dreadful blow he has been dealt!

NOAH

Left my . . . left my . . .

NOAH AND GRANDMA AND GRANDPA GELLMAN

Chanukah GELT

NOAH

All that money!
Twenty dollars!

GRANDMA AND GRANDPA GELLMAN

Twenty dollars!
In your pocket!
In the pocket of your pants!

NOAH

In the pocket of my pants!
There's still a chance!
Maybe she hasn't done the laundry!
There's all that cleaning after a party.
Oh please clock please clock
strike three now.

GRANDMA AND GRANDPA GELLMAN

Tick tock tick tock.

NOAH

Anyhow
she can't—it's MINE!
She can't have my money! I'll sue!
Aw come on clock!

GRANDMA AND GRANDPA GELLMAN

It's only two.

I'm plotzing with anxiety!

GRANDMA AND GRANDPA GELLMAN
All right already; now it's three.

NOAH
(Rushing home:)
FINALLY!
The second I hear the three o'clock bell
—I'm a bat out of hell!
I run down the street—like a blur!
and right away,
the washing machine!

THE WASHING MACHINE
Consequences unforeseen!
I'm on!

NOAH
In the basement! It's on! It's HER!
The spin cycle's already started to spin!
She's down there! Wait! Wait! CAROLINE!

(Noah rushes into the basement.)

CAROLINE
What?

NOAH
Did you find . . . ?

(Little pause.)

CAROLINE
Yup.
I did.
And now it's mine.

NOAH

No. It's mine. I'll tell Daddy.
I'll tell Rose!

CAROLINE

You left that money in your clothes,
easy comes and easy goes.

NOAH

Give it back!
It isn't fair!

CAROLINE

You think I care?
Don't shout at me!
I found this money in your pocket.
Your mama says I gets to keep it.

NOAH

(Getting frantic:)
No she didn't! Pocket change!
She never said you could have my present!
Twenty Dollars! Give it! Mine!
Twenty Dollars!
Twenty Dollars!
Twenty Dollars!
Twenty Dollars!

CAROLINE

Go Noah, scram, out of my face!
Don't leave your money all over the place.
Now I can take my boy to the dentist!
Now I can buy real presents for Christmas.
The twenty's mine, now go away,
ain't nothin but money, you gots plenty,
rules are rules!

NOAH

Give it back! STOP IT! *NO NO NO NO NO NO!*

CAROLINE

Noah you stop it, calm yourself! CALM!

CAROLINE	NOAH
CALM!	CAROLINE!
CALM!	GIVE IT BACK!
CALM!	CAROLINE!
	I HATE YOU! I HATE YOU! I HATE YOU!
	There's a bomb!
	President Johnson has built a bomb
	special made to kill all Negroes!
	I hate you, hate you, kill all Negroes! Really! For true!
	I hope he drops his bomb on you!

(Pause.)

CAROLINE

Noah, hell is like this basement,
only hotter than this, hotter than August,
with the washer and the dryer and the boiler
full blast, hell's hotter than goose fat,
much hotter than that.
Hell's so hot it makes flesh fry.
(Little pause.)
And hell's where Jews go when they die.
(She gives Noah the twenty.)
Take your twenty dollars baby.
So long, Noah, good-bye.

(Caroline leaves.)

10.

AFTERMATH

Some time later that day, Rose enters, laden with grocery bags.
Noah, alone in the basement, puts the twenty in the bleach cup. The
Dryer is still singing.

ROSE

Hello I'm back!
Back from shopping!
Caroline? Noah! Is anyone home?

(Noah emerges from the basement.)

ROSE

Noah help Grandpa with the groceries.
Where's Caroline, darling?

NOAH

Caroline left.

ROSE

She left?

NOAH

Yes.

ROSE

Why? Is anything wrong?

NOAH

No, she just left.

ROSE

With the laundry still on?

*(Rose goes into the basement. She switches off the Dryer.
She returns to the kitchen.)*

ROSE

Noah, is there something you aren't telling me?

*(Noah runs off past Mr. Stopnick, entering, grocery-laden.
Noah goes back to the basement:)*

NOAH

And the next day day day Caroline stayed away-way-way
and she didn't come back back back and she didn't come back
   back back.
And the next day day day Caroline stayed away-way-way
and she didn't come back back back and she didn't come back
   back back.
On the third day day day Caroline stayed away-way-way
and she didn't come back back back and she didn't come back
   back back.

*(Stuart is now home, playing the clarinet. Rose, in the basement, finds
the twenty in the bleach cup. She goes upstairs to Stuart. Mr. Stopnick
enters and listens.)*

TONY KUSHNER

ROSE

Stuart, I'm worried,
she left in a hurry,
I call her at home,
she won't come to the phone,
her kids say she's out,
but I have my doubts.
I think she's there;
this isn't like her.

(Rose waits, Stuart plays.)

ROSE

Stuart!

(He puts down the clarinet.)

STUART

Maybe she's ill.

ROSE

And look, in the bleach cup:
a twenty dollar bill.

(Noah enters.)

ROSE AND STUART

Noah please, no monkey biz:
Tell us whose this twenty is.

(Noah doesn't respond.)

STUART

Noah?

ROSE

Did Caroline find this money in your pants?

(Little pause.)

MR. STOPNICK

No, Rose, I think the twenty is mine.
I thought I'd lost it.

(He takes the twenty back.)

MR. STOPNICK

Now everything's fine.

(Noah returns to the basement.)

NOAH

And the fourth day day day Caroline stayed away-way-way
and she didn't come back back back and she didn't come back
    back back.
(Little pause.)
I did it. I killed her. I did it she died.

(Rose is on the telephone:)

ROSE

Dotty? Rose Gellman.
Is Caroline—Oh.
Well why didn't she call and tell me so?
I'm glad she's fine but—
I've been worried, a lot,
I couldn't imagine,
for five days and not—
If she needed time off,
if it's family stuff,
and things around here have been
sort of tough,
well, not tough, more like tense,
but it doesn't make sense,

to just up and vanish without an adieu,
I thought maybe she'd gotten the Spanish flu.
Tell her to call.
That's all that I ask,
I won't take her to task,
just tell me what's what.
I worry a lot.
Thanks, Dotty.
You're swell.
(She hangs up.)
You can all go to hell!
I'm not the enemy!

MR. STOPNICK

No, you're the boss.

ROSE

Oh shut up, Papa. Forget it. Her loss.

STUART

I have to go practice.

(They look at him.)

ROSE

Great. Thanks a lot, Stu.

STUART

No, really, I do.

MR. STOPNICK

So what else is new?

(A look between Mr. Stopnick and Stuart. Stuart leaves the room. His clarinet can be heard in the room adjoining.)

MR. STOPNICK

Here's how I see it.

ROSE

I didn't ask.

MR. STOPNICK

Nonetheless. You want that boy to love you.

ROSE

I guess, yes of course. And I've tried!
At bedtime he'll only let Stu tuck him in,
if I try to do it—well, somehow I blew it!

MR. STOPNICK

And his mother is dead—

ROSE

Forget it!

MR. STOPNICK

And everything's wrong,

ROSE

No-win.

MR. STOPNICK

Then you marry his father but you don't belong.

ROSE
But how he misses Caroline—
Caroline!

MR. STOPNICK
Caroline.
Given the givens, she's in
    perfect position
for the boy to adore her.
She's competition.

ROSE

Competition! Oh, yes! And I *meant* to destroy
the silly attachment of that little boy
for the maid.
Oh I'm the oppressor, right? I'm the employer!

MR. STOPNICK

I don't mean you consciously planned to destroy her
in Noah's affections—

ROSE

OK fine.

MR. STOPNICK

Well, not by design.
But maybe you had to—
one way or another.
It's hard, but not mean.
You got in between.
Maybe Rosie, now you can be his mother.

ROSE

It figures you figure in three seconds flat
how to make me the villain—

MR. STOPNICK

I didn't say that.

ROSE

I'm glad you came down, now go home, keep in touch.
You've made me feel awful, thanks ever so much!
And while you were giving me this third degree
perhaps you neglected to notice that he
still won't let me near him—so I've failed.

MR. STOPNICK

. . . Wait and see.

ROSE

Just stop it Papa, stop picking a fight!

MR. STOPNICK

I didn't mean to upset you, Rosie. Honor bright.

(He kisses her and leaves.)

ROSE

I'm not the boss.
(Shrugs.)
Her loss.
Leave it be and let it end.
It's just no way to treat a friend.

11.
LOT'S WIFE

Dotty in front of the Thibodeaux front porch. Caroline is dressed in her Sunday church clothes.

DOTTY

Mornin Caroline.

CAROLINE

Morning Dot.

DOTTY

How you doin, girl? Doin all right?

CAROLINE

I can't visit now, it's gettin late.

DOTTY

Mrs. Gellman call,
looking for you.
(Little pause.)
You ought to call her, say you quit.

CAROLINE

I ain't said I quit.

DOTTY

Ain't been to work there
for five days, honey;
that sure sound like quit to me.

CAROLINE

Oh I got to go to church, Dot.
I need to pray.
Said and done some things this week I'm sad about.
I need to pray.

DOTTY

Caroline, Emmie is young, she don't know about you,
about what you'd do if you'd a mind to.
Change yourself, Caroline,
learn something new!
Show her your fire, show her your grit,
show her your new face.

CAROLINE

And what? What should I do?

DOTTY

Call the Gellmans and quit?

(Little pause.)

CAROLINE

And then my three childrens can beg for they feed.
Dot, I need . . .
Dot. It too late.

DOTTY

I never seen you so sad.
We known each other all these years.

TONY KUSHNER

Caroline, my heart bleed for you,
but folk can't just surrender to their fears.
I know it hurt to change.
It actually hurts, learning something new,
and when you full-grown, it's harder, that's true—
it feel like you got to break yourself apart,
it feel like you got to break your own heart,
but
folk do it. They do.
Every day, all the time,
alone, afraid, folks like you.
You got to let go of where you been.
You got to move on from the place you're in.
Don't drown in that basement. Change or sink.
Let go, forget, move on.
This ain't time for prayin. You got to think.

CAROLINE

I'm going to church
and I'm going to pray.
And from now on, only God hear what I have to say.
Cause only God can hear what my heart mean to state.
When I talk to people, all that comes out is hate.
Cause I hate. That all.
I hate.
I know what I'm doin, Dot.
I need nothin from you.
I want you to go.
Out my yard.
(A beat.)
We through.

DOTTY

Well I heard that.
Take care.
I'll get out of your hair.

You go on and pray.
Tell God Dotty say hey.
Tell Him I'm doin perfectly fine.
Sure is a pleasant Sunday. Mornin,
Caroline.

(Dotty leaves.
Caroline is alone.)

CAROLINE

Sixteen feet below sea level.
Caught tween the Devil and the muddy brown sea . . .

That money . . .
That money . . .
That money reach in and spin me about,
my hate rise up, rip my insides out.

My madness rise up in a fury so wild and I let myself go.
Spoke my hate to a child.
Pennies done that. Pennies done that.
Pocket change . . .

Pocket change change me, pocket change change me,
can't afford loose change, can't afford change,
changin's a danger for a woman like me,
trapped tween the Devil and the muddy brown sea.
I got to get back to the way that I been
God!
Drag me back to that basement again.
Don't know what I said to that little boy . . .

Always they's been people who
hold they head high gettin through.
I can't.
Ain't never been no good,

116

findin joy the way you should,
hopin water turn to wine—
hope's fine
hope's fine
hope's fine—
till it turn to mud.
And some folks goes to school at nights,
some folks march for civil rights.
I don't.
I ain't got the heart,
I can't hardly read.
Some folks do all kinds of things and
black folks someday live like kings
and someday sunshine shine all day!
Oh sure it true
it be that way
but not for me—
This also true:
ya'll can't do what I can do
ya'll strong but you ain't strong like me:

I'm gonna slam that iron
down on my heart
gonna slam that iron
down on my throat
gonna slam that iron
down on my sex
gonna slam it
slam it
slam it down
until I drown
the fire out
till there ain't no air left
anywhere.
What else
what else
what else

what else God
what else God give me an arm for?

SLAM go the iron
SLAM go the iron
FLAT!
FLAT!
FLAT!
FLAT!

Now how bout that then?
That what Caroline can do!
That how she rearrange herself,
that how she change!

Murder me God down in that basement,
murder my dreams so I stop wantin,
murder my hope of him returnin,
strangle the pride that make me crazy.
Make me forget so I stop grievin.
Scour my skin till I stop feelin.
Take Caroline away cause I can't be her,
take her away I can't afford her.
Tear out my heart
strangle my soul
turn me to salt
a pillar of salt
a broken stone and then . . .

Caroline. Caroline.

From the evil she done, Lord,
set her free
set her free

set me free.

Don't let my sorrow
make evil of me.

*(Jackie and Joe enter from the house, dressed for church. They come
down the porch steps and run past Caroline. She stops them, inspects
their clothes, tidies them up. They run off.*

*Emmie, dressed for church and carrying Caroline's hat, coat, purse
and gloves, sullenly hands them to her mother.*

*Caroline takes her things; as Emmie starts to leave, Caroline grabs
her and pulls her into a fierce embrace.*

*Caroline releases Emmie, who walks away, after her brothers.
Caroline puts on her hat and follows Emmie, going to church.)*

12

How Long Has This Been Going On?

Salty
       Salty
              Salty
Salty teardrops
           Teardrops
                   Teardrops
I been spillin salty teardrops in the ocean.
Uh oh oh oh oh
Salty
       Salty
              Salty
Salty teardrops
           Teardrops
                   Teardrops
I been cryin salty teardrops under water.
I'm lookin for answers Lord
                   High above, in the clouds
Askin you tell me now

Why I cry out loud

How long?
How long?
This been goin on?
(Uh uh oh)
How long?
How long?
This been goin on?
Nothing
           Nothing
                      Nothing
Nothing happens
                    happens
                              happens
Nothing happens under ground
in Louisiana,
cause there is no under ground,
                              in Louisiana
no there ain't no under ground
                              in Louisiana
there is only
            there is only under water
oh-oh-oh
there is only
            there is only
under water.

(While the Radio is singing:
Caroline, in her maid's uniform, on the porch of her house. She's smoking
a cigarette, listening to the Radio.
Noah is in his bed in the Gellmans' house. Rose is standing at the
doorway of Noah's bedroom.)

NOAH

Why does our house have a basement?
Under ground is under water.

This is where the Great Plains end
in the Gulf of Mexico.

ROSE

Go to sleep now, go to sleep.

(She starts to leave.)

NOAH

Rose?

(She stops and turns. He's never called her back before.)

ROSE

Noah?

NOAH

If there's only water under ground,
is my mother buried under water?

ROSE

Don't be silly, she's safe and sound,
they buried her above the ground,
in a dry little house;
not even a mouse can get in, I bet.
Listen, your daddy's clarinet . . .

*(Rose kisses Noah good night. Noah lets her. Downstairs, Stuart plays
a blues-y clarinet. Rose joins him.
Noah leans out the window.)*

NOAH

Good night, Caroline.

CAROLINE

Go to bed Noah, stop botherin the night.

NOAH

I'm glad you came back to work today.
Sorry I hid from you.

CAROLINE

Someday you won't.
Someday we'll talk again.
Just gotta wait.

NOAH

Will we be friends then?

CAROLINE

Weren't never friends.

(In the sky above, and in the Gellmans' basement below:)

THE MOON
Household rules and small
    decrees,
unsuspecting bring us these

secret little tragedies.

THE WASHING MACHINE
Household rules and small
    decrees
unsuspecting bring us these
costly, quiet victories.

NOAH

Caroline?

CAROLINE

Mmmmm?

NOAH

What's it like under water?

CAROLINE

Under water?

It's like a song you hear on the radio at night.
Like sleepin with the light out.
It's like the wooden sound of your mama sad bassoon.

Noah,
Someday we'll talk again
but they's things we'll never say.
That sorrow deep inside you,
it's inside me too,
and it never go away.
You be OK.
You'll learn how to lose things . . .

My sorrow go where my heart grow calm.
When you stop breathing air you get
oh so calm,
no fire down there
so it's calm calm calm
and there's never any money
so it's very very calm
but you miss
oh you miss
the sun and the moon
and the wooden bassoon.

NOAH

And sharing cigarettes?
(Little pause.)
Do you miss sharing a cigarette?

CAROLINE

You bet I do, Noah,
you bet, you bet.

EPILOGUE
EMMIE'S DREAM

Caroline puts out her cigarette.

THE MOON

Mornin, mornin in the air,
silver sparkle on the green.
World awaken to prepare
for the consequence unforeseen.

(Emmie has appeared on the lawn in her nightgown. Caroline looks at her, then goes inside, giving her daughter the stage.)

EMMIE

Just one last thing left unsaid:
Who was there when that statue fell?
Who knows where they put his head?
That ol copper Nightmare Man?
Who can say what happened that night at the courthouse?
I can.

I was there that night; I saw,
I watched it topple like a tree.
We were scared to death to break the law!
Scared to fail, scared of jail.
But still we stayed—

And I said:
"Statue, statue
you are through!"
Statue answer: "Well who are you?"
I said: "Evil, you got to go!"
Evil answer: "Who says so?"
I say:
"Emmie
Emmie Thibodeaux!

"I'm the daughter of a maid,
in her uniform, crisp and clean!
Nothing can ever make me afraid!
You can't hold on, you Nightmare Men,
your time is past now on your way
get gone and never come again!
For change come fast and change come slow but
everything changes!
And you got to go!"
Shout shout Devil on
out!!

(Jackie and Joe come out on the porch in their pajamas.)

JACKIE AND JOE

Sssshhhh!
Mama sleepin, she work all day.
Don't wake Mama, let her sleep,
let her dream till the mornin come.
She been workin hard . . .

EMMIE

I'm the daughter of a maid.
She stands alone where the harsh winds blow:
Salting the earth so nothing grow
too close; but still her strong blood flow . . .
Under ground through hidden veins,
down from storm clouds when it rains,
down the plains, down the high plateau,
down to the Gulf of Mexico.
Down to Larry and Emmie and Jackie and Joe.
The children of Caroline Thibodeaux.

THE END